IN THE
BEGINNING

Genesis

N E L S O N

I M P A C T ™

Bible Study Series

IN THE BEGINNING

Genesis

THOMAS NELSON
Since 1798

NASHVILLE DALLAS MEXICO CITY RIO DE JANEIRO

A Word from the Publisher…

*Be diligent to present yourself approved to God, a worker who does not need
to be ashamed, rightly dividing the word of truth.*

2 Timothy 2:15 NKJV

We are so glad that you have chosen this study guide to enrich your biblical knowledge and strengthen your walk with God. Inside you will find great information that will deepen your understanding and knowledge of this book of the Bible.

Many tools are included to aid you in your study, including ancient and present-day maps of the Middle East, as well as timelines and charts to help you understand when the book was written and why. You will also benefit from sidebars placed strategically throughout this study guide, designed to give you expanded knowledge of language, theology, culture, and other details regarding the Scripture being studied.

We consider it a joy and a ministry to serve you and teach you through these study guides. May your heart be blessed, your mind expanded, and your spirit lifted as you walk through God's Word.

Blessings,

Edward (Les) Middleton, M.Div.
Editor-in-Chief, Nelson Impact

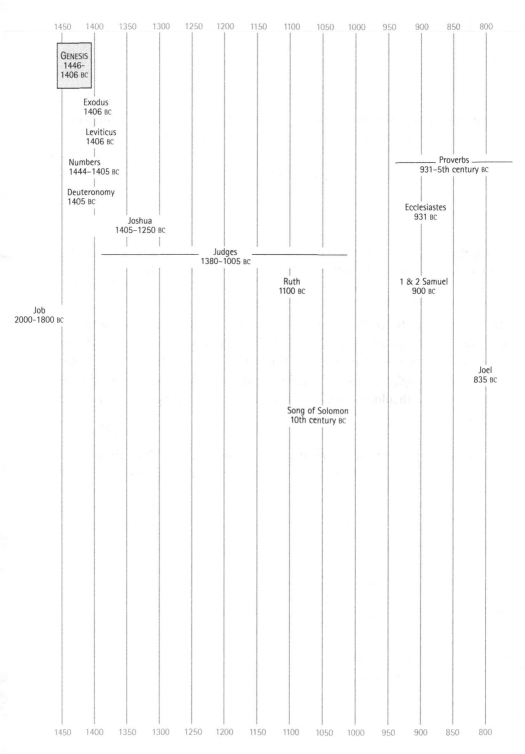

| 1450 | 1400 | 1350 | 1300 | 1250 | 1200 | 1150 | 1100 | 1050 | 1000 | 950 | 900 | 850 | 800 |

GENESIS
1446–
1406 BC

Exodus
1406 BC

Leviticus
1406 BC

Proverbs
931–5th century BC

Numbers
1444–1405 BC

Deuteronomy
1405 BC

Ecclesiastes
931 BC

Joshua
1405–1250 BC

Judges
1380–1005 BC

Ruth
1100 BC

1 & 2 Samuel
900 BC

Job
2000–1800 BC

Joel
835 BC

Song of Solomon
10th century BC

| 1450 | 1400 | 1350 | 1300 | 1250 | 1200 | 1150 | 1100 | 1050 | 1000 | 950 | 900 | 850 | 800 |

TESTAMENT WRITINGS

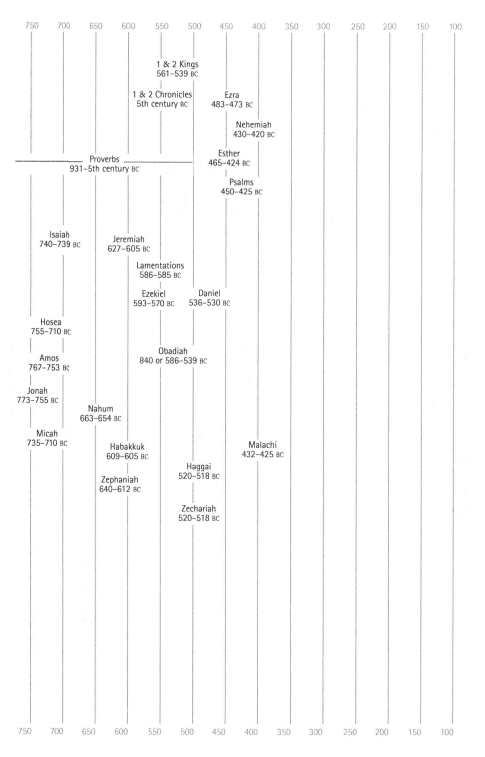

| 750 | 700 | 650 | 600 | 550 | 500 | 450 | 400 | 350 | 300 | 250 | 200 | 150 | 100 |

1 & 2 Kings
561–539 BC

1 & 2 Chronicles
5th century BC

Ezra
483–473 BC

Nehemiah
430–420 BC

Esther
465–424 BC

Proverbs
931–5th century BC

Psalms
450–425 BC

Isaiah
740–739 BC

Jeremiah
627–605 BC

Lamentations
586–585 BC

Ezekiel
593–570 BC

Daniel
536–530 BC

Hosea
755–710 BC

Obadiah
840 or 586–539 BC

Amos
767–753 BC

Jonah
773–755 BC

Nahum
663–654 BC

Micah
735–710 BC

Malachi
432–425 BC

Habakkuk
609–605 BC

Haggai
520–518 BC

Zephaniah
640–612 BC

Zechariah
520–518 BC

| 750 | 700 | 650 | 600 | 550 | 500 | 450 | 400 | 350 | 300 | 250 | 200 | 150 | 100 |

OLD MIDDLE EAST

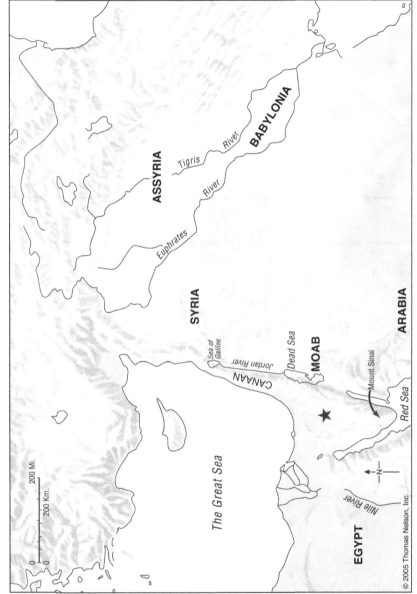

★ The book of Genesis was written in the wilderness south of Canaan.

MIDDLE EAST OF TODAY

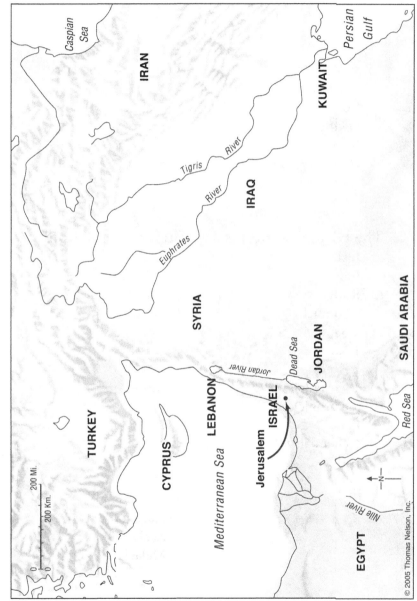

OLD TESTAMENT DIVISIONS

The Pentateuch
Genesis
Exodus
Leviticus
Numbers
Deuteronomy

Wisdom Literature
Job
Psalms
Proverbs
Ecclesiastes
Song of Solomon

The Historical Books
Joshua
Judges
Ruth
1 Samuel
2 Samuel
1 Kings
2 Kings
1 Chronicles
2 Chronicles
Ezra
Nehemiah
Esther

The Prophetic Books
Isaiah
Jeremiah
Lamentations
Ezekiel
Daniel
Hosea
Joel
Amos
Obadiah
Jonah
Micah
Nahum
Habakkuk
Zephaniah
Haggai
Zechariah
Malachi

New Testament Divisions

The Four Gospels
Matthew
Mark
Luke
John

History
Acts

The Epistles of Paul
Romans
1 Corinthians
2 Corinthians
Galatians
Ephesians
Philippians
Colossians
1 Thessalonians
2 Thessalonians
1 Timothy
2 Timothy
Titus
Philemon

The General Epistles
Hebrews
James
1 Peter
2 Peter
1 John
2 John
3 John
Jude

Apocalyptic Literature
Revelation

ICON KEY

Throughout this study guide, you will find many icon sidebars that will aid and enrich your study of this book of the Bible. To help you identify what these icons represent, please refer to the key below.

BIBLICAL GRAB BAG

A biblical grab bag full of interesting facts and tidbits.

BIBLE

Further exploration of biblical principles and interpretations, along with a little food for thought.

LANGUAGE

Word usages, definitions, interpretations, and information on the Greek and Hebrew languages.

CULTURE

Customs, traditions, and lifestyle practices in biblical times.

ARCHAEOLOGICAL

Archaeological discoveries and artifacts that relate to biblical life, as well as modern-day discoveries.

CONTENTS

INTRODUCTION

THE ULTIMATE BEGINNING

Before We Begin . . .

What person, event, or concept first comes to mind when you think of Genesis? Can you explain why?

It may be easy to name the first person who is introduced in Genesis, but how about the person whose story brings the book of Genesis to a close?

Who were the first three patriarchs of the Nation of Israel?

Choose the one person in the following list whose name is not mentioned in Genesis:

Seth	Abraham	Lamech	Enosh	
Laban	Moses	Rachel	Reuben	Rebekah

To speak of the book of Genesis without using the word *beginning* would be a remarkable feat, roughly comparable to reciting every word Shakespeare ever wrote, walking on your hands from New York to Nashville, and then squaring the circle. All in one day, of course.

Why? The reason is quite simple. We all use the word *beginning* in many contexts and situations—the beginning of a romance, the beginning of a career, a new day, a new trip, or a new game of chess. Writers and editors even talk about the beginning of a sentence, a paragraph, or a book. Boring, perhaps, but also revealing. For all such beginnings tend to be important to someone.

What has been the most significant "beginning" in your life?

On the other hand, no person on Earth can escape the significance of the "quest for beginnings" that mankind has been on ever since . . . well . . . *that* beginning! The one that started everything. The beginning that eventually led to Charles Dickens, chocolate ice cream, and chapels on the tops of hills.

And that particular beginning is also referred to within the opening words of the book of Genesis: "In the beginning God created the heavens and the earth." What could be more central to human existence?

WHAT'S IN A NAME?

The Hebrew title of the book we call Genesis comes from the very first word in the original Hebrew text, which would be transliterated into English as *Beresheit* (bare-a-sheet), and translated into English as "in the beginning." The corresponding Greek word is *geneseos,* as in verse 2:4, from the early Greek translation known as the Septuagint, which said, "This is the book of the geneseos of heaven and earth."

esu WHAT MAKES HEBREW EVEN HARDER . . . ?

The original text of the Bible not only used no vowels but also did not include separations between the words. Is it any wonder, then, that a reference book such as *Gesenius' Hebrew-Chaldee Lexicon to the Old Testament* sometimes contains a whole page of possible meanings for a given word? Is it also surprising that scholars are still not unanimous about the precise meaning of some passages? Truly, the wonder of modern scholarship is the degree of unanimity in the translations we have today, not the relatively few disputations!

Thus, long ago we derived our English name for a Hebrew book from a Greek word—and arrived at Genesis.

Jews and Christians alike believe that Genesis, along with the next four books of the Bible, were all written at the Lord's direction by the greatest human hero of both religions, Moses. However, even though this view has generally been considered correct by most experts down through the centuries, it has come under fire from various sources.

For example, some scholars have argued that Genesis (along with the next four books of the Bible, together forming what Christianity calls the "Pentateuch") was actually written by the prophet Ezra, who has his own book later on.

If true, that would move the composition of Genesis forward several thousand years, to a time when the Jews had begun returning to Jerusalem from captivity in Babylon. That would date it to 458 BC, or later. On the other hand, the written "Law of Moses" is referred to in very clear terms at least twenty times in other historical books of the Bible. More telling still, it was referred to on eight separate occasions, in the *New King James Version* of the Bible, in descriptions of historical events that happened long before Ezra's birth.

In other words, Ezra hadn't even been born when the "Law of Moses" became familiar enough to be referenced several times in historical accounts that predate Ezra. And though the "Law" portion of the Pentateuch did not really begin in Genesis, the first five books of the Bible are so much a "unity" (what the ancient Hebrews might call an *echad*) that it's almost impossible to imagine the first book being written thousands of years after the others, by someone who—righteous as Ezra was—did not talk directly with God and get his information firsthand, as Moses did.

Others have suggested that Moses had neither the literary training nor the free time to write anything as detailed yet comprehensive as Genesis and the next four books. This view, of course, completely overlooks the role of God Himself in Moses' enablement. It also contradicts the New Testament words spoken by Stephen in Acts 7:22: "And Moses was learned in all the wisdom of the Egyptians, and was mighty in words and deeds (NKJV)."

esu WHAT IS TRANSLITERATION?

Hebrew is one of the few languages in the history of the world that works on both a pictographic and an alphabetic level. Most languages are one or the other—Chinese, for example, is pictographic, meaning that the thousands of "pictures" each have meanings and spoken sounds of their own. But the pictures are not combined into a succession of sounds that "spell out" longer words.

The pictographs of the Hebrew language also have built-in meanings of their own, but their initial sounds (such as the sound of "d" in the Hebrew picture/letter "dalet") are also combined into "sound bites" that yield Hebrew words. This means that the letters in a Hebrew word give readers both its pronunciation and the concepts behind its meaning.

Thus the word *shomer* (pronounced show-mare) is made up of the letters that yield the sounds of *sh, m,* and *r.* (Vowel sounds are sometimes indicated by dots and dashes below the letters, or are left out entirely, as they were in the biblical text, and simply "understood.") The pictographic meaning of the word *shomer,* based on the "pictures" built into the letters, might be translated as "one who holds back chaos." In English, the equivalent word is most often "watchman."

Also, the word we spell here as *beresheit* could just as legitimately be spelled *berasheet, bearusheat,* or even the "sound-spelling" used earlier, *bare-a-sheet.* For even though the name for our alphabet (which experts tell us comes from the first two letters of the Greek alphabet, *alpha-beta*) sounds remarkably like the first two letters of the Hebrew alphabet (*aleph-bet*), those two letters look nothing like our own *a* and *b.*

The bottom line is that Hebrew is a rich language capable of conveying vast concepts in very few words. The downside is that it is so rich in potential meaning that it can be very hard to translate into English words on which everyone can agree.

In Hebrew, much more so perhaps than in any other language, context is everything.

Bigger Than the Universe . . .

In overall span, the book of Genesis begins with the origin of the universe and proceeds to a point in time approximately 4,000 years before the birth of Christ. Along the way it moves from the story of creation to the introduction of sin into the heart of newly minted humankind. Sin arrived via the fallen angel the ancient Hebrews knew by the title "Ha'Satan," or "the adversary." From this it is easy to see where the name *Satan* came from.

Genesis then tells us a series of fascinating stories—of Cain and Abel, the Tower of Babel, and the Great Flood, to name just a few. As the waters finally began to recede, God promised Noah that He would never destroy the Earth by water again. He then set the first rainbow in the sky as a visible reminder of His pledge.

A short time later we meet Abram, the "friend of God" (James 2:23 NKJV) with whom the Lord soon established an eternal covenant. In the process, He changed Abram's name to Abraham, and promised that Abraham and his descendants, through his wife, Sarah (whose name God also changed from Sarai), would forever be known as God's Chosen People.

In the following chapters we meet Isaac and Rebekah, then Jacob and Rachel, and eventually all twelve of their sons. The book of Genesis ends at chapter 50 with the death of Joseph, Jacob's second-youngest. By then, all of Joseph's brothers, whose descendants later became the twelve tribes of Israel,

esu What Is the Septuagint?

The Septuagint is the earliest known Greek translation of the Hebrew Scriptures. It originated in Egypt between 300 and 200 BC. Modern scholars believe that as many as seventy-two Jewish scholars collaborated to produce it—hence its name, which means "seventy" in Latin.

had joined Joseph in Egypt. Soon they became slaves to the Egyptians. Unable to break free on their own, they eventually received a miraculous deliverance, provided and directed by God but "project managed" at ground level by Moses.

Christians and Jews alike believe that Moses, like Joseph before him, was "planted" among the Egyptians long before his moment in history came, to give him access to everything he would need. Only God, of course, could bring about such long-range plans, both then and now. In due time, of course, we will talk about these things in greater detail, for Moses has not yet been introduced when the book of Genesis draws to a close.

"I AM THE LORD YOUR GOD . . ."

This precise phrase appears forty-one times, word-for-word, in the *New King James Version* of the Bible, always in the Old Testament and always attributed to the Lord Himself. The same word-for-word phrase also appears an average of thirty-seven times each in four other popular Bible translations. The slight difference in frequency can be accounted for by minor differences in translation, but either way the importance of this understanding cannot be overestimated. God clearly wanted us to know that He was and is the absolute sovereign over all creation—and that He is our God!

GREATER THAN THE MIND OF MAN . . .

The Bible makes no attempt whatsoever to deal with the origin of God. Thus, "In the beginning God" must surely be the most profound statement in history, and also the most self-evident. Centuries later, David pointed out that "the heavens declare the glory of God," but by then the first verse of Genesis had already beaten him to the punch. Surely nothing can compare with the power and majesty of that magnificent opening statement.

The same words also introduce us to an awesome concept. The Bible must never be taken lightly. The minute one takes it for granted, he or she will miss something. A certain critic once spoke of writers who "peek over the top of their words." God, of course, doesn't need to peek over the top of anything, yet there He is in the first four words of Genesis, perhaps with a twinkle in His eye, challenging us to catch what He just said.

How does that one phrase—"In the beginning"—represent a central building block of the Christian faith?

God simply is. Unlike us, He has no need to explain Himself; no need to examine or expound on His motives; no need to paint His own picture and wear it in a cameo around His neck. In fact, it really isn't until Exodus 34:6–7, eighty-four chapters and almost two books later, that God confirms what readers of the Bible could largely discern on their own at that point. That's when He finally tells Moses what His nature truly is.

Meanwhile, within the book of Genesis itself, God clearly establishes several truths of a theological nature.

1. First, that He is the Creator of the universe.

2. Second, that He always was, is, and shall be the sovereign Lord over His creation.

3. Third, that He will have His will even if He has to move heaven and earth to get it.

4. Fourth, that He would prefer to bless humanity, but . . .

5. Fifth, that He will not overlook disobedience and unbelief to give us false assurance.

IS IT MARS OR MARS?

The names for planets such as Mars and Jupiter, all of which were created as part of "the heavens," are always capitalized while the name for our own planet, Earth, often is not. Gradually, we have begun to use a lowercase *e* even when we are clearly talking about "the whole thing" as a solar entity, which was once the standard for capitalization.

The question is, will the rules of "equal opportunity" and "equal treatment" eventually extend to the rest of our solar system, so that someday an astronaut who died on mars will be buried under the mars of the planet mars? Or, before we get to that point, will there be an intermediate state in which future generations will speak of the "earth of mars"?

In fact, it is especially important to understand something else, something deeper, with respect to #5. A thorough reading of the Bible should convince us that it's not really a question of God's willingness to deal with our sin. He is so willing He even offered His own Son as a sacrifice to cover those sins! God cannot pretend that sin, in any form whatsoever, is ever okay.

This is true for one simple reason—our God is a holy God. Because of that limitless holiness, sinful people cannot enter into His presence and remain alive. Pure holiness literally destroys sin. Thus, in Moses' time, a mere priest could become like kindling to the fire if he failed to completely purify himself before entering God's literal presence in the Most Holy Place, deep within the tabernacle in the wilderness. Once inside, He had to be very careful to "minister before the Lord" exactly as He had been instructed by God. That's why the ministering priest wore bells in the hem of his garment, and a rope around his ankle. He did the first so they could hear him moving (and know if he stopped!), and the second so they could pull his lifeless body out if he failed in any way.

Again, that's not in Genesis. Neither, of course, is the story of God's Son, Jesus Christ, by whose life, death, resurrection, and constant intercession on our behalf we no longer need to go through anything involving blood sacrifices and brass altars. But of course, we're getting ahead of ourselves again! (Yet, when you're reading a great story, maybe it's sometimes a good thing to know a bit about the ending in advance.)

If the book of Genesis ever gets hard to understand—or if the nature of God ever seems too much to comprehend—we must remember that the Bible is a complete package. More of God's mystery and magnificence does unfold as we move farther into His Book.

Genesis, after all, is just the beginning . . .

THE GODLY PATTERN . . .

It seems clear that God established a definite pattern very early in the creation process. In creating the universe, He first created the raw materials and then refined them into something far more orderly and functional, in a step-by-step fashion. When all else was accomplished, He then refined some of the dust of the earth into the first man. Next He took a rib from the man to fashion a woman.

Likewise, God has allowed (and even encouraged) humanity to work with the raw materials of the earth to refine metals, to extract and combine other natural materials, and eventually to fabricate everything we now take for granted in the modern era, from medicines to computers.

To extend the pattern to a spiritual plane, soon after God had created a perfect man and a perfect woman and had given them dominion over a perfect earth, He stepped back into the picture and created a way for humanity to be rescued from the chaos of sin. Likewise, He will eventually step back in on both a spiritual and a physical plane and rescue us one final time.

THE CREATION

GENESIS 1:1–2:3

Before We Begin . . .

In the beginning, the earth was without form—a void. What statement by God changed the disorder into order and the emptiness into fullness?

Within the first seventeen words, the book of Genesis introduces four concepts that should make the entire world sit up and take notice.

FOUR BASIC TRUTHS

1. First, in addition to being what we have already called an extremely profound statement, "In the beginning God" could well be the most underestimated in the Bible, as well. When we look at the sentence as a whole ("In the beginning God created the heavens and the earth") it's possible to glide completely over the significance of those first four words.

   In the beginning . . . God! There was nothing before Him; everything that is or ever will be came after Him.

2. Second, God created everything out of nothing. In the original Hebrew, the word used for "created" was *bara* (and was actually the second word in the Hebrew original), which is reserved for God alone. No one else can create matter where none existed before, and nowhere in the Bible does this word reference the acts of anyone but God.

3. Third, God created all. "The heavens and the earth" takes in all that is—what we commonly call the universe. Thus God is also the undisputed sovereign over everything that exists, for the creator is always superior to the thing created.

4. Fourth (and this truth can be drawn from all the above), right there in the first few verses of His own Book, God defined and established, once and for all, the foundation of all the other laws He gave to Moses on Mount Sinai, and thus to all of humanity: "I am the Lord your God."

The Bible tells us that God created everything by simply speaking the words. For example, He said, "Let there be light." But what language did He use?

ALL IN A DAY'S WORK

The question of what a "day" constituted, in the first chapter of Genesis, has intrigued humanity for thousands of years. Was it a 24-hour time span, an entire geological age, or something in between? The Hebrew word *yom*, which was used here in Genesis, referred to a 24-hour period of time throughout the remainder of the Old Testament. But that fact, by itself, is not conclusive proof. Did it mean something else when it was used here?

To complicate things, we know that God exists "outside of time" and is not constrained by it in any way. How else, for example, could He orchestrate the mailing of a check on Monday, which you prayed for on Tuesday, to arrive on Wednesday?

So, was God working "within Earth time" when He created the universe, or was He not? What do you think?

WHAT TIME IS IT?

God's description of the days of the week, in Genesis, gives rise to the ancient Hebrew understanding of a "day" as beginning at one sundown and ending at the next. However, considering that sundown begins at different times in each daily cycle, depending on the seasons, very few days by that reckoning would be precisely 24 hours long.

To make it more complicated, a "day" in one part of the world would not correspond to a "day" in another part because of a host of other factors. These would include the relative positions of the sun and the Earth at various times of the year. And, of course, the precise location of any particular spot on Earth would also be a factor—"days" at the equator are not quite equal to "days" at either of the poles.

All of these factors made it a bit dicey for the ancient Hebrews to determine exactly when certain of their sacred feast days, as ordained later in the Bible by God, should actually begin and end. They eventually evolved a unique system of signal fires and trumpet blasts, relayed from Jerusalem outward to the surrounding towns, to let everyone know when certain times had officially arrived.

Ironically, even though we now have atomic clocks and defined time zones, our system for telling time is just as arbitrary as it ever was. The whole thing depends on agreements between people that "This is how we'll do it." In fact, in some cities in the United States it is possible to cross the street, go from one state to another, and lose an hour, all in the same second of "real" time!

THE SEQUENCE OF CREATION

Once we move past the opening verses of Genesis we begin to get the details of creation itself. The following list shows the main events only, in order as they happened, as detailed in Genesis from the third verse of chapter 1 through the second verse of chapter 2.

First Day

1:3–4—God created light and divided it from darkness.
1:5—God called the light Day and the darkness Night.

Second Day

1:6–8—God made the firmament and separated the waters of Earth from those in the atmosphere.
1:8—God called the firmament Heaven.

Third Day

1:9—God gathered the waters of Earth together and commanded dry land to appear.
1:10—God called the dry land Earth, and called the waters Seas.
1:11–12—God created grasses, herbs, and fruits.

Fourth Day

1:14–17—God created the sun, the moon, and the stars, and set them in the heavens.

Fifth Day

1:20–21—God created all sea creatures and birds.
1:22—God blessed all the above and told them to "Be fruitful and multiply."

Sixth Day

1:24–25—God created all the beasts of the earth.
1:26–27—God created man in His own image, then gave him dominion over all fish, birds, and living things on the earth.
1:28—God blessed man and told him to "Be fruitful and multiply; fill the earth and subdue it," having dominion over all living things as described above.
1:29–30—God said that He had given man every seed-yielding herb and every seed-yielding fruit as food.

SEVENTH DAY

2:1–3—On the seventh day God ended His work, rested, and both blessed and sanctified ("set apart") that day.

Do you observe a "sabbath"—a day of rest, reflection, and worship? If so, what do you do?

Previously, we said that the ancient Israelites used a system of "trumpet blasts" and signal fires to communicate from group to group. What various forms of "signaling" are used in our society to signify the beginnings and endings in our worship services?

Note how, in the complete biblical text, in addition to the "godly pattern" mentioned elsewhere in this chapter, God also used essentially the same creation sequence each time:

1. First, He spoke the appropriate words.
2. Second, He told us the result.
3. Third, He called it "good."
4. Fourth, in some cases He gave names to what He had created.
5. Fifth, He indicated when each day ended via the "evening and the morning" comment.

Also Worth Noting . . .

God Himself explained that He created and positioned the celestial bodies (primarily the stars but also the planets and other bodies, too) to serve as signs for seasons and days and years. Because of their relatively fixed positions (even though the stars themselves actually do move in their own individual orbits), the stars have also been used for navigation since ancient times. For centuries, no commander of a sailing vessel dared to venture onto the open sea without knowing how to "shoot the stars" and figure out where he was.

As Psalm 19:1 makes clear, the wonders of heaven were also put in place in a way that purposely displayed the handiwork of God. Thus we could have no doubt of the wondrous nature of our Creator. The only thing they were definitely not put there for was to be worshiped in place of God Himself. Sadly, in the name of astrology, men and women have done so from ancient Babylonian times right down to the present day.

The Bible tells us that man was made "in the image of God." At the same time we are told that God is spirit and doesn't have a "regular" or "constant" physical form (although, obviously, He could take on any physical form He wanted anytime He wanted to, as Christ did when He came to live among us). Thus we have to assume that "image" refers to His attributes, His essential nature, which we were meant to emulate within our own spirits so that we could have spiritual fellowship with Him. These attributes, incidentally, will be discussed in greater detail as we move farther into the Bible and examine more of God's communications with humanity.

Much has been written about God's establishment of the seventh day as a day "set apart" for rest. God also blessed it and made it holy . . . but why? Certainly He Himself didn't need "rest" per se. He never sleeps because He never gets tired! Thus the correct answer is undoubtedly twofold. First, we do need physical rest. But second (and more important), we truly need to dedicate a definite amount of time each week to focusing on God, learning more of Him, and worshiping Him to the best of our ability. In that way we can be refreshed both physically and spiritually.

Psalm 19:1, mentioned earlier, tells us: "The heavens declare the glory of God; And the firmament shows His handiwork" (NKJV). What are some things in our world that declare the handiwork of God—from the visible, physical "things in the heavens" to those things that are invisible or unseen by our eyes?

PULLING IT ALL TOGETHER . . .

• The first verse of Genesis establishes God's preeminence above all else. Only He was "in the beginning." The first verse says that He created everything out of nothing. The first verse also proclaims that God created all. The remainder of this portion of the book of Genesis (Gen. 1:1–2:3) gives a straightforward accounting of God's creation of the world.

• The final three verses of this portion tell us that God purposely rested on the seventh day, both blessing and setting apart that day for that specific purpose.

2

Sin Enters a Perfect World

Genesis 2:4–4:26

Before We Begin . . .

What people or events first come to mind when you think of the book of Genesis?

What principles do you tend to connect with those same people or events?

This section of Genesis begins with a striking example of a Hebrew stylistic technique that is not always familiar to readers of English translations. We are accustomed to thinking in linear terms. We expect a narrative to begin at the beginning (as in chapter 1 of Genesis) and then proceed in a straight line, with each event recorded in succession. This is how Western authors write the majority of our textbooks, novels, and news accounts.

Much of the time the Bible uses the linear model, too, but it does not always record historical events in strict, straight-line fashion. In chapter 2, verses 4–7 give us a superb example of a typical recapitulation (or "recap"), in which the author briefly summarizes what has gone before. In this particular case, verse 4 makes it very clear that "This is the history of the heavens and the earth when they were created, in the day that the Lord God made the earth and the heavens . . ." (Gen. 2:4 NKJV).

The next three verses then complete this brief summary, ending by recapping the creation of Adam, even though we have already read about it earlier:

And the LORD God formed man of the dust of the ground, and breathed into his nostrils the breath of life; and man became a living being. (Gen. 2:7 NKJV)

It's almost as though God, through Moses as His scribe, wanted to make absolutely sure that we were right there with Him, listening carefully as He unfolded the story of creation before He went on to the next subject.

Of what significance is it that God Himself breathed life into man only? Why not into the other animals, as well?

In what respects was man made "in the image of God"? Does this mean that we literally look like God Himself?

THE GARDEN OF EDEN

Next, God begins the last two acts of His creation as recorded in Genesis—except that He is no longer creating "from nothing." Now He begins refining elements of what He had already brought forth. First He set apart a beautiful home for Adam, called the Garden of Eden. He then filled it with every tree that is "pleasant to the sight and good for food" (Gen. 2:9 NKJV).

The exact location of the Garden of Eden remains a mystery, although most scholars believe it was positioned northwest of the Persian Gulf. The four rivers mentioned in Genesis 2:10–14 included the Euphrates and probably what we now

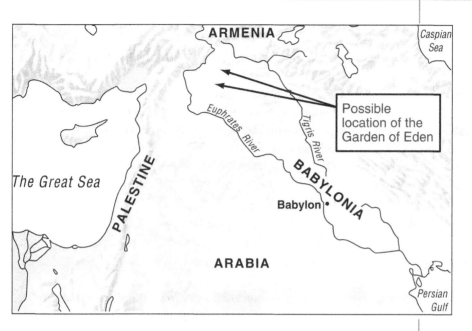

call the Tigris, as well. The Garden might have been located between these two rivers, in part of an area called the "fertile crescent" that extended from the eastern shore of the Mediterranean Sea to the Persian Gulf. This area has also been called the "birthplace (or cradle) of civilization." Its Greek name, *Mesopotamia*, meant "land between the rivers."

In Genesis 2:15, God put Adam in the Garden, to "tend and keep it." He also instructed Adam, very clearly, that he could eat of every tree in the Garden except one, the tree of the knowledge of good and evil, "for in the day that you eat of it you shall surely die" (Gen. 2:17 NKJV). He then brought all the animals before Adam and allowed him to name each one.

At that point God either realized or simply acknowledged, as a way of explaining what He was about to do, that Adam needed companionship. This is when He put Adam to sleep, extracted a rib, and fashioned Eve, literally, from Adam's own body. Adam then called her Woman "because she was taken out of Man" (Gen. 2:23 NKJV). At that point God also established the institution of marriage, both sanctifying it in the lit-

DOES GOD "REALIZE GRADUALLY" OR DOES HE JUST "KNOW"?

The jury is still out on whether God created Eve after He realized that Adam needed companionship. Some believe that Eve was in God's divine plan all along, even before Adam came into being. Granted, the text of Genesis 2:18 has God saying, "It is not good that man should be alone; I will make him a helper comparable to him" (NKJV). But did these thoughts come to God as new information of that moment, or was He simply expressing what He already knew would be true, along with His perfect solution?

eral "setting apart" sense and giving it His obvious blessing:

> *Therefore a man shall leave his father and mother and be joined to his wife, and they shall become one flesh. (Gen. 2:24 NKJV)*

Why do you think God created man before He created woman? Why not the other way around?

God obviously recognized our human need for companionship. What does His deliberate creation of a companion for Adam tell us about the importance of living in community with others?

GOD AS THE MASTER TEACHER

As we read through the Bible, we discover that God knew a great deal about how the human brain works. Genesis 2:4–7 is one of the earliest-occurring examples. Here we are, barely one full chapter into Genesis, and already God is (1) reviewing what has happened so far, (2) restating the concepts He wants to be sure we understand, and (3) setting us up for a clear understanding of the next series of events.

Later on, the vision of Ezekiel in which he saw a man measuring the temple, is an even more striking example of what we now call "multi-sensory" teaching. Ezekiel saw the measurements being taken, heard them being spoken, and then wrote them down.

The Bible's obvious awareness of how people learn is not surprising, of course, for God designed and built our mental faculties Himself.

ENTER THE WILY SERPENT . . .

In the centuries that have gone by since God put Adam and Eve in the Garden of Eden, millions of words have been written about what happened next, with all its profound theological, cultural, and moral implications. Genesis records the complete story, including the universal and eternal consequences, in chapter 3. Here are some thoughts to keep in mind as you read through the verses.

1. Eve herself has often been blamed for what happened, but let's be fair. The serpent was actually Satan himself, at once the most evil and one of the most clever beings in the universe. In her innocence, Eve was simply no match for him. This was his big chance to ruin the paradise God had created. If Satan hadn't been able to fool Eve in the manner he first chose, surely he would have tried something else—and probably many more deceptions until he found one that worked. The history of the world since that time shows that he had barely begun to reach into his bag of tricks. (See also "Was It Really Eve's Fault?" on the following page.)

2. To help put the above into perspective, Christ Himself was also tempted by Satan. He won the battle of wits by quoting God's own Word, but Eve didn't have the same weapon. She had only her memory of what God had forbidden her and Adam to do. Now, whether she purposely chose to disregard what she knew to be true is an open question . . . but then Adam would have to answer the same question, too, for he soon joined her in eating the forbidden fruit.

3. God's immediate actions, and the judgment He brought against Adam and Eve, involve many subtle nuances. Here are just three . . .

   a. God sacrificed an animal to provide clothing for Adam and Eve, symbolically covering their sin. Later on, He would require similar sacrifices from the children of Israel to cover their sin—essentially a life for a life. The connection of this concept to the atoning sacrifice of Christ Himself is equally clear and direct.

   b. Adam (and thus all of humanity) was formed from dust. Rather than living forever in a sinless state, Adam (and Eve—and all of us) would now return to dust.

WAS IT REALLY EVE'S FAULT?

Genesis 2:15 tells us that God put Adam in the Garden of Eden to "tend and keep it." However, modern Bibles do not convey the full meaning of the Hebrew word translated as "keep"—it also meant to guard or protect. But what would Adam need to protect the Garden from, if not the beasts of the field (Gen. 2:20 NKJV) that had no reason to be in it? And was not the serpent a "beast of the field" with no rightful place inside the Garden?

Thus we could make the case that Adam's own failures left the door open for Eve's downfall. First, he failed to keep the serpent outside. Second, he left Eve alone to fend for herself, which is when she got into trouble.

Whose fault was it, anyway?

c. Other aspects of Adam and Eve's existence were also forever changed. For example, all women would now bear children in pain, and all men would now earn their bread by the sweat of their brows.

4. Note that the Bible does not tell us that Eve actually had a name of her own, and had just been called "the woman," until Genesis 3:20. There we are told that "Adam called his wife's name Eve [*Chava*, in Hebrew], because she was the mother of all living" (NKJV). This is probably another example of the Bible's occasional non-linear nature. At the very least, it seems unlikely that Adam would choose that precise moment, between God's judgment on him for his sin and his resulting expulsion from the Garden, to give his wife a name.

EVIL BY ANY OTHER NAME . . .

Because of their pictograph/letter combinations, ancient Hebrew names had intrinsic, "built-in" meanings of their own. In an almost literal sense, a person "was" his name. Later on we'll encounter some examples of names that God purposely changed, to make them fit their bearers a little better. But one of the earliest name changes occurred off-line and is not specifically recorded in the Bible.

The Hebrew text of the Bible refers to the evil being we call Satan as "Ha'Satan" (sometimes transliterated without the apostrophe), meaning "the adversary." As the Bible records in greater detail later on, Ha'Satan began as one of the archangels who surrounded God's throne. When the soon-to-be-Satan archangel led the rebellion that got him thrown out of heaven, God also stripped away his proper name. He thus symbolically removed his identity, as well. Ha'Satan then became the title from which we synthesized the name Satan, and that's how we know him today.

There has been much speculation down through the centuries, but no one knows for certain what his original name actually was. However, it clearly was not Lucifer. This was his Babylonian name, as quoted in Isaiah 14:12, but never the name by which He was known by God.

How do you believe the world—and mankind itself—might have evolved if sin had not entered into the picture?

CAIN KILLS ABEL

The first few verses of chapter 4 give us the familiar account of Cain and Abel. It might be hard to find any story in the Bible that has been repeated more often, to more diverse audiences, than this short, abrupt tale of unprovoked killing, the first of more than thirty instances of murder in the Bible. The story contains a number of interesting "threads," any of which you might pursue at length. For example . . .

1. To use the wording of the *New King James Version* of the Bible, why did God "not respect" Cain's offering? Was it because it was not a blood offering, which is mainly what the Lord required of the Israelites many years later? Or, was there something inherently inferior, or second class, in the actual fruits Cain offered? And one more possibility—did it have anything to do with Cain's attitude?

2. Obviously Cain was angry, but why did he take it out on Abel? Was it simple blind jealousy, unrestrained and spilling over? Or, crude as this might seem, was Cain in effect saying to God, "You want a blood sacrifice? All right—I'll give you a blood sacrifice!"

3. What did God mean when He told Cain, in Genesis 4:7, "If you do well, will you not be accepted? And if you do not do well, sin lies at the door. And its desire is for you, but you should rule over it" (NKJV). What criteria was God referring to when He spoke of "doing well" and "being accepted"?

4. Cain also initiated the world's first cover-up when he attempted to avoid responsibility for what he had done, via the famous "Am I my brother's keeper?" question. In other words, one sin leads quickly to another, each one easier than the first.

5. No one has ever been able to positively identify the "mark of Cain" that God put upon him to protect him from the vengeance of others. Some say it was an actual physical mark of some kind, while others claim it was an attitude or a demeanor that inspired pity. What do you think?

Why do you think God chose to protect Cain, even after what he did?

DEATH BY ROCK OR BLADE?

The Hebrew word *harag*, meaning to "slay or slaughter," was used in the Bible for what Cain did to Abel and what Lamech did to his unknown victim. However, the same word also connotes ritual slaughter, as in the blood sacrifices God required of Israel later on. These required a sharp knife and a skillful stroke, to bring about a rapid and complete draining of the blood—a death which, ghastly as it sounds, is actually very quick and painless (and is the method still used by kosher butchers, incidentally, which is much more humane than many other methods).

Even so, most readers of the text seem to assume that Cain killed Abel with a rock. But why not a knife? How else, in fact, to account for the words of God in Genesis 4:10: "The voice of your brother's blood cries out to Me from the ground" (NKJV). Was this reference to blood literal or metaphorical? And if it was literal, how much blood might a fatal blow from a rock actually bring forth?

In a larger sense, chapter 4 is about the rapid spread of godlessness into other parts of the known world of that era. For without God as its focus, ruler, and source of inspiration, the world fell quickly into degradation. One of the best examples of this is the ancient story of Lamech, seventh in succession from Adam himself.

First, Lamech defied God's original intent for one man to be married to one woman as "one flesh," and took a second wife. He then killed a young man merely for wounding him, by implication an accidental offense that could have been as slight as a mere bumping together of their two bodies. Nonetheless, Lamech extracted the ultimate penalty. Worse yet, he boasted about it to his two wives and then demanded of God a far more lenient treatment than anything Cain might have received. And Cain, of course, was his role model, for Lamech was simply following in Cain's footsteps, indulging his own evil instincts by striking out and harming others.

CAIN WAS FIRST BUT NOT LAST!

Cain's killing of his brother, Abel, was the first murder recorded in the Bible, but certainly not the last. Other well-known examples would include:
- Pharaoh's killing of Israelite male infants, of which Moses was miraculously spared.
- Moses' own slaying, years later, of an anonymous Egyptian.
- David's arranging for the death of Uriah, Bathsheba's "inconvenient" husband.
- Joab's killing of David's son Absalom as he hung by his hair from a tree.
- Jezebel's killing of the prophets of the Lord.
- Herod's murdering of all infants two years old and under in Bethlehem and the surrounding area, in a vain attempt to kill Christ.
- Herodias's request for the head of John the Baptist, and John the Baptist's subsequent murder in Herod's prison.
- The martyrdom of Stephen.

Chapter 4 then concludes on a positive note with the birth of Seth to Adam and Eve. In the words of his mother, Seth was appointed by God as "another seed for me instead of Abel, whom Cain killed" (Gen. 4:25 NKJV).

To Seth was then born Enosh, at which point "men began to call on the name of the Lord" (Gen. 4:26 NKJV). Certainly a hopeful ending for the fourth chapter of Genesis!

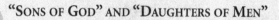

"SONS OF GOD" AND "DAUGHTERS OF MEN"

Many generations of biblical scholars have struggled to understand the exact meaning of Genesis 6:1–4. Some claim that the "sons of God" were literally fallen angels who were part of the rebellion led by Satan, who came to earth and mated with human women. Others claim that those who "came in to" the daughters of men were ordinary humans, possessed by demonic spirits. It is well beyond the scope of this guide to examine these events in detail, but many supplementary resources, in the form of detailed commentaries and, indeed, entire books, are available to anyone who wishes to do further research.

One such reference includes the book of Enoch, which was part of the Hebrew Bible in Jesus' time but was taken out by the council of Constantinople in the sixth century AD.

PULLING IT ALL TOGETHER . . .

• God created the first man, Adam, out of the dust of the earth.

• God created the first woman, Eve, from a rib taken from Adam's body.

• God established a home, first for Adam by himself and then for Eve as well, in the Garden of Eden. Its probable location was somewhere northwest of the Persian Gulf.

• Sin then entered the world when Satan disguised himself as a serpent and tricked Eve into defying a specific commandment from God Himself. But Adam did the same, at her urging, and thus shared in her guilt. Indeed, it was Adam to whom God directed His initial inquiry into what had happened.

• Adam and Eve were thus driven from the Garden and condemned to lives of pain, suffering, and eventual physical death, none of which were part of God's original plan for humanity.

• Cain committed the first murder by killing his brother, Abel. Not long afterward, Lamech killed a man for "wounding" him, and thus the cycle of physical violence, one man or woman against another, began to spread throughout the world.

3 NOAH AND THE FLOOD

GENESIS 5:1–9:29

Before We Begin ...

What is your understanding of why the Flood came about?

Does what happened seem unfair to you? Why or why not?

When they read the portions of the Bible that deal with genealogy—such as the fifth chapter of Genesis—people sometimes ask why that information was important enough to be included in the Bible. Boring? Maybe. But consider three possible reasons why this information is included:

First, the Bible is the world's most important historical record. It simply cannot afford to be vague about such matters. Consider just one example: Christ was the promised Messiah, to be born of the "house of David." But how could we know who His family was without a meticulous accounting of all His earthly ancestors?

Second, God has many ways of reinforcing the points He wants us to remember. The extraordinary lifespan of the first few generations of man—as compared to ours—gives us a striking contrast between perfect man as God created him and fallen man as he got farther and farther away from the Garden of Eden. By embracing sin, Adam and his descendants lost their physical perfection.

Third, of those whose children and "years on earth" are listed, we are clearly told (with the exception of Enoch) that each one died. Might this not be another subtle reminder of what comes from sin?

Note also how chapter 5 concentrates on the lineage of Seth, the son God gave to Adam and Eve after Abel. As we move forward in history, the differences between the descendants of Seth and those of Cain, listed in chapter 4, become more and more clear. Neither line was perfect, but the last verse of chapter 4 tells us:

> And as for Seth, to him also a son was born; and he named him Enosh. Then men began to call on the name of the Lord. (Gen. 4:26 NKJV)

And then, a few generations later, came Noah.

esu A CUBIT BY ANY OTHER NAME . . .

The ancient measurement known as a cubit was roughly equal to 18 inches in length, or one-and-a-half feet. So, 10 cubits would be 15 feet long and 100 cubits would be 150 feet long. Thus Noah's ark, at 300 cubits, would be about 450 feet long, the length of one-and-a-half football fields. It would be 75 feet wide (50 cubits times 1.5). Surprisingly, those two measurements are remarkably similar to the proportions of modern ocean liners. Or, perhaps we should say that modern vessels are remarkably similar to the ark!

NOAH BUILDS THE ARK

The exact nature of all the events recorded in Genesis 6:1–7 are not entirely certain, but one thing is quite clear. Even though men were calling on the name of the Lord when Enosh was born, by the time of Noah's birth—eleven generations after Adam (which does include a man named Lamech, by the way, but not the same Lamech who descended from Cain and also committed murder)—the earth was completely

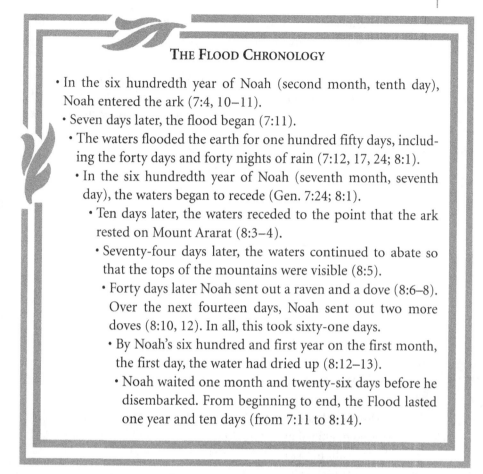

THE FLOOD CHRONOLOGY

- In the six hundredth year of Noah (second month, tenth day), Noah entered the ark (7:4, 10–11).
- Seven days later, the flood began (7:11).
- The waters flooded the earth for one hundred fifty days, including the forty days and forty nights of rain (7:12, 17, 24; 8:1).
- In the six hundredth year of Noah (seventh month, seventh day), the waters began to recede (Gen. 7:24; 8:1).
  - Ten days later, the waters receded to the point that the ark rested on Mount Ararat (8:3–4).
  - Seventy-four days later, the waters continued to abate so that the tops of the mountains were visible (8:5).
  - Forty days later Noah sent out a raven and a dove (8:6–8). Over the next fourteen days, Noah sent out two more doves (8:10, 12). In all, this took sixty-one days.
  - By Noah's six hundred and first year on the first month, the first day, the water had dried up (8:12–13).
    - Noah waited one month and twenty-six days before he disembarked. From beginning to end, the Flood lasted one year and ten days (from 7:11 to 8:14).

"corrupt before God, and the earth was filled with violence" (Gen. 6:11 NKJV).

Except, of course, for Noah, to whom God spoke directly in chapter 7, giving him explicit directions for building the ark that would save his family, plus pairs of all the animals on earth at that time. When all were inside, God Himself then sealed the ark and the rains began. Water also came from the "fountains of the great deep," which probably included underground rivers and springs that broke through to the surface.

In addition, huge reserves of trapped water might have been freed by the shifting of earth's crust underneath the seas themselves, causing the oceans to rise precipitously even without the rain from above.

Discussing the Flood can bring about powerful images in our minds of recent natural disasters that have occurred on earth. How does being confronted with tragedy of this magnitude make you feel?

How might it cause you to view God?

HOW MANY ANIMALS DID NOAH TAKE?

Most people seem to think that Noah took one pair (a male and a female) of every kind of animal on earth into the ark with him. But if that were true, how could he then afford to sacrifice (or eat) any animals at all when the flood was over? Wouldn't each killing effectively wipe out an entire species?

The answer is that God instructed Noah to take one pair of each unclean animal, and seven pairs of each clean animal.

In all, within forty days the earth was completely covered by water, to the very tops of all the mountains, and every living land creature on earth perished except for those who were in the ark with Noah. The question that then arises is, why would God go to such extreme lengths? Did not the Flood amount to "cruel and unusual punishment"? Here are some points to consider:

First, the Flood demonstrates God's ultimate and eternal power over His creation. Nothing in the universe can stand against Him and prevent Him from executing His judgment and His will, no matter how proud, defiant, or mighty it might become.

Second, the Flood demonstrates God's utter and complete hatred for sin, and His willingness to do whatever He deems necessary to counteract evil when it goes too far.

Third, the Flood demonstrates that, even as God always deals with sin on His own unchanging terms, He also provides salvation for those who love Him and follow His commandments.

These three points are greatly condensed—like all great stories of the Bible, the Flood itself can provide a separate "flood" of insights into a great number of God-versus-man considerations!

HOW DID NOAH KNOW WHAT HE KNEW?

After the rains stopped and the dry land reappeared, Noah sacrificed some of the extra animals he'd brought aboard the ark. But since God did not give His law to Moses until many years later, when the Israelites reached Mt. Sinai in their escape from Egypt, how did Noah know which animals were clean (i.e., suitable for both eating and sacrificing) and which were not?

This is one of the mysteries of the Bible, though not as "unsearchable" as some. Obviously the Bible could not record every single happening, and just as obviously, though we tend to think of the giving of the law to Moses as a first-time event, God must have made many things clear to the earlier patriarchs.

AFTER THE FLOOD

No one knows with absolute certainty where the ark eventually came to rest 150 days after the rains began. The Bible simply tells us that it settled "on the mountains of Ararat" (Gen. 8:4 NKJV), which scholars believe would be in what is now eastern Turkey. But so far we have only speculation about the ark's actual location.

After waiting several days, Noah began sending out a dove as a scout. The first time the bird returned with nothing, and the next time it returned with a freshly plucked olive leaf in its beak. The third time it did not return at all, which Noah took as a sign that the earth was now dry enough to walk upon again.

And so, more than 200 days after the ark found its eventual home (and after more than a year inside the ark), Noah, his wife, his three sons, their wives—eight people in all—and all the animals finally set their feet on dry land again.

How do you imagine that Noah and his family spent their days on the ark?

Notice what happened next:

> *Then Noah built an altar to the Lord, and took of every clean animal and of every clean bird, and offered burnt offerings on the altar. . . . Then the Lord said in His heart, "I will never again curse the ground for man's sake, although the imagination of man's heart is evil from his youth; nor will I again destroy every living thing as I have done." (Gen. 8:20–21 NKJV)*

HAS NOAH'S ARK BEEN FOUND?

Through the years a number of claims have been made to the effect that Noah's ark has at last been found. Books have been written, TV shows have been produced, and thousands of people have been convinced that various expeditions to the Ararat region of eastern Turkey had finally found definite proof. Alas, none of these reports have panned out. In more than one case, what were first touted as "convincing photographs" turned out to be photos of ordinary rock formation. If any identifiable physical parts of Noah's ark still remain, they are elusive.

What was basically the first thing Noah did when he came out of the ark?

God further responded in three additional ways:

First, He blessed Noah and his sons. Second, He charged him to be "fruitful and multiply." Third, He established a covenant with Noah in which He promised never again to destroy the earth by water.

He also sealed the covenant with a sign by which to forever remind Himself of His promise—the world's first rainbow!

Do you ever think of God's covenant with Noah when you see a rainbow? Do you think it still means the same thing today as it did to Noah?

THE CURSE OF CANAAN

Exactly what happened next has puzzled biblical scholars for generations, and they are still not in total agreement. However, we know for certain that Noah planted a vineyard, made wine, and got drunk. Eventually he went to sleep and lay naked in his tent. The Bible then tells us that Ham "saw the nakedness of his father, and told his two brothers outside" (Gen. 9:22 NKJV), and this is where the misunderstandings begin.

His brothers responded by taking a garment, holding it between them, walking backward into the tent, and covering their father with it. But that didn't fix things, for when Noah woke up he "knew" that Ham had seen him naked and thus pronounced the "curse of Canaan" against him, while adding a corresponding blessing on Ham's two brothers, Japheth and Shem.

WHAT IS IT ABOUT 40?

For some reason the number 40 has been associated in the Bible with several people and events. Consider the following:

Noah	40 days of rain
Moses	40 years of exile in Midian
Moses	40-day fast on Mt. Sinai
Israelites	40 years of wandering in the desert
Israelite Spies	40 days of espionage in Canaan
Nineveh	40 days to repent
Elijah	40-day fast on Mt. Sinai
Christ	40-day fast and temptation
Christ	40 days on earth after His resurrection

Is there a connection between all these 40s?

What does all this mean? To begin with, we know that seeing your father naked amounted to a violation of the family ethic of ancient times. It simply was not done; to do so, even by accident, would be essentially "mocking" the father. In modern terminology, we might say this "disrespected" Noah. Thus Ham did not need to engage his inebriated father in any "sexual" way, as some have suggested. Neither did he need to sleep with his mother or commit any other sexual transgressions against his father, as others have also suggested. Just seeing Noah naked was enough.

It appears, however, that Ham made things worse by telling his two brothers what he'd seen. The immediate result was a curse on Ham's descendents, the Canaanites; thus Ham's actions dishonored his own family for many generations. At the same time, the lines of both Shem and Japheth were blessed by Noah. And, all three pronouncements by Noah (called an "oracle" by scholars) were proven abundantly true in the centuries ahead.

What might be considered modern-day ways of "mocking" one's parent(s)?

PULLING IT ALL TOGETHER . . .

• The life spans of men in early biblical times were extremely long. However, as people got farther and farther away from their sinless origins, life spans got shorter and shorter.

• The descendants of Seth, Adam's "Abel-replacement" child, vacillated between righteousness and paganism. Eventually, Noah and his small family were the only righteous people on Earth.

• God then destroyed the earth—and all the evil in the hearts of people that flourished up to that time—by water. But evil began to return even in Noah's time, even though humanity got a fresh start after the Flood.

ABRAHAM AND THE COVENANT

GENESIS 10:1–21:32

Before We Begin . . .

What do you recall about the chief lesson of the story of the Tower of Babel?

The next twelve chapters of Genesis cover a lot of territory, so we'd best begin!

Chapter 10 gives us what is commonly called the "Table of Nations." This amounts to a brief survey of where Noah's descendants settled after the Flood. However, it is not like the genealogy tables in chapters 5 and 11, for both of those are vertical listings that concentrate on who descended from whom. Chapter 10 gives us a horizontal listing, showing where in the ancient world the sons of Noah went as they fulfilled the Lord's command to be fruitful and multiply.

Note that Ham's descendents wound up in the land of Canaan, as we mentioned previously. We will meet them again, many times, in the books and chapters ahead—and as a rule they won't be any more pleasing to the Lord than Ham was to Noah!

THE TOWER OF BABEL

The story of the Tower of Babel, told in Genesis at the beginning of chapter 11, is one of the more familiar tales in the Bible. A group of ancient people, recently arrived in the Plain of Shinar (now modern Babylon), thought they could build a tower all the way to heaven and thus be on an equal footing with God Himself. But God was not pleased with their arrogance. Soon He stepped in to stop their building and move most of them out of the area into other parts of the world.

Even so, as often as we might have heard this story, its deeper lessons are not always obvious to us. Here are some things to think about:

It would seem that God's words to Noah in Genesis 9:1 were very clear: "Be fruitful and multiply, and fill the earth" (NKJV). However, one of the things we have had trouble remembering, since Adam's days in the Garden, is that God says what He means and means what He says. The tale of the Tower of Babel provides a graphic illustration of what happens when we hear and do only half of what God requires. "Be fruitful and multiply" was easy, but apparently "fill the earth" was not.

The same story also provides another of those "chronological variations" common to ancient Hebraic writing, as mentioned at the beginning of chapter 3 of this guide. The dispersal of Noah's sons is detailed in chapter 10, but the main event that brought much of that dispersal about is told "after the fact" in chapter 11.

The simplest explanation is that Moses wrote it that way to lay out more clearly the parallels between the ancient people of Babylonia and the Israelites themselves, thousands of years later. In either case, the only thing the people who eventually became the Babylonians really had to do was listen to God and do what He said. But pride continually gets in the way. And, as always, God tends to visit humility on those who cannot find it within themselves.

Thus pride built a tower intended to reach all the way to heaven. And thus the Builder of heaven Himself knocked down that tower and scattered its builders across the face of the known world of that era, to "fill the earth" as He'd commanded. The giving of separate languages was a simple device meant to ensure their separation, one group from another, in a manner that only a truly supreme being could do.

Think how difficult it is for some of us to master foreign languages over long courses of study. Yet God gave a whole series of brand new languages, to thousands of people at once, in the twinkling of an eye!

Why do you think the people did not obey God's command to "fill the earth"? What might they have been afraid of?

In what ways do we build "towers" today?

What is the connection between the Tower of Babel and our commonly used word babble?

The remainder of chapter 11 is another genealogy, again a vertical listing showing a straight line from Shem to Abram. This list extends the line that went from Adam, to Seth, to Noah . . . and thus to the "founding member" of the Nation of Israel.

What is the ultimate covenant that God repeatedly says He wants to enter into with His people?

THE STORY OF ABRAHAM, PART ONE: A RIGHTEOUS MAN

The story of Abraham can be broken down many different ways, but let us consider it in four main chunks, and let us then look at a few of the highlights from each of those arbitrary divisions.

First of all, chapter 12 opens with the following verses, in which Abraham is still called by his original name, Abram:

> *Now the Lord had said to Abram:*
> *"Get out of your country,*
> *From your family*
> *And from your father's house,*
> *To a land that I will show you.*
> *I will make you a great nation;*
> *I will bless you*
> *And make your name great;*
> *And you shall be a blessing.*
> *I will bless those who bless you,*
> *And I will curse him who curses you;*
> *And in you all the families of the earth shall be*
> *blessed." (Gen. 12:1–3 NKJV)*

This passage shows how far the Lord was willing to go to establish a righteous relationship with Abram. Abram had only to obey—to go to the land that God promised to show him. In return, God promised blessings that are still part of Abraham's heritage to this day, including the well-known promise to "bless those who bless you" and "curse him who curses you."

Why do you suppose God chose Abraham, of all the people on earth, to establish a covenant and bless his descendents forever?

Two Ancient Covenants

The Bible gives us very few details about the nature of the various well-established covenants that were part of the ancient Hebraic culture, but it does give us several examples. The most basic of these was known as the service covenant, but was more commonly called blood a covenant because of the way in which it was established. Genesis 15:9–21 gives us the most detailed example in the Bible, when God entered into a blood covenant with Abraham. Essentially, the parties to a blood covenant sacrificed an animal, cut it into pieces, and passed between the pieces. This signified that they agreed to accept the same punishment (i.e., death and dismemberment) before they would break the terms of the covenant.

The second of these covenants was known as the friendship covenant but was more commonly called salt covenant, because it was established by mixing salt from each of the participants together in a common bowl. The covenant could then only be broken if the participants could each take back his or her own grains of salt.

Some commentators believe that this was the type of covenant Abram and Melchizedek established with each other, signified by the breaking of bread and the probable sharing of salt. To this day, for practicing Jews, part of the evening meal that ushers in the Sabbath involves eating salted bread. A more detailed example of what it can mean in "real life" can be found in the relationship between David and Jonathan that occurred many years later. David honored the terms of their covenant long after Jonathan died. He went out of his way to find Jonathan's son, Mephibosheth, then brought the boy into his own household and cared for him as though he were his own son.

The story of David's kindness to Jonathan's son is told in 2 Samuel, chapter 9. This same eternal covenant is also mentioned many verses later, in 2 Samuel 21:7, where it once again motivated David to save Mephibosheth's life.

Next, we find Abram in the land of Egypt, where he'd gone to escape a famine. Here, because he thought the Egyptians might harm him so they could take his beautiful wife away, Abram instructed Sarai to let their hosts believe that she was his sister instead. This would not be the last time this particular deception would be practiced by Abraham or his descendants, but it ended well. God prevented anyone who might have been inclined to claim Sarai as his own wife from doing so. Abram was then asked to leave the country when the true nature of their relationship became apparent.

In chapter 12 we see Abram and his nephew, Lot, struggling in the land of Canaan to peacefully coexist. They had both prospered so much that their herds were too big for the land to support. Thus came the division that sent Lot eastward, while Abram stayed where he was.

At this point, the Lord spoke to Abram again, adding the following specifics to the promise He'd made before:

> *Lift your eyes now and look from the place where you are—northward, southward, eastward, and westward; for all the land which you see I give to you and your descendants forever. And I will make your descendants as the dust of the earth; so that if a man could number the dust of the earth, then your descendants also could be numbered. (Gen. 13:14–17 NKJV)*

ABRAM THE WARRIOR

The first section of chapter 14 now shows us, once again, the nature of humanity, with one ancient group of people warring against another exactly as people have done ever since. It also demonstrates the nature of ancient covenants between various groups. Among other things, covenants were roughly equivalent to nation-to-nation treaties of today. If two countries were in covenant together and one was attacked, the other would be honor-bound to fight on their behalf, and vice versa.

Eventually, some of these warring groups took Abram's nephew captive (here, Lot was called Abram's "brother" in the Hebrew text), along with all his goods. At that point Abram demonstrated that he must have known something about fighting, as well, for he soon led a successful campaign to rescue Lot and restore his possessions.

Next comes one of those incidents in the Bible that can seem puzzling at first, but only because it's not an easy matter to understand all the relationships involved. In verses 17–24 of chapter 14, we meet both the king of Sodom and Melchizedek, the king of Salem. Here is a brief explanation of why Abram dealt with each one as he did:

First, even though the king of Sodom made an appealing offer, Abram refused to keep for himself any of the Sodomite goods that he'd captured in the battle he'd just won. Knowing what he already did about the king of Sodom, Abram wanted no long-term linkages whatsoever—no favors given or received—to come due at some later date.

Second, Abram paid a tithe to Melchizedek, king of Salem, which later became Jerusalem, the capital city of God's chosen people. Melchizedek can seem like one of the more enigmatic figures in the Bible, for he appears out of nowhere, has no known ancestry, and shares bread and wine with Abram (see "Salt Covenant" elsewhere in this chapter). He is also mentioned several times in the remaining books of the Bible—once in Psalm 110 and eight times more in the book of Hebrews, where he is often understood to be a "type" of Christ.

Look at it this way: Because Abram paid him a tithe, we know that Melchizedek was a high priest, worthy of Abram's homage. We also know that he was of a higher order than the Levitical priests who came much later, for they descended from Abram and could therefore not be superior to him.

Beyond that, consider how David referred to Christ Himself in Psalm 110:4: "You are a priest forever according to the order of Melchizedek" (NKJV). Clearly there is more going on here than meets the eye—you are encouraged to do further research if your curiosity is aroused!

THE STORY OF ABRAHAM, PART TWO

ETERNAL COVENANT

We now see Abram interacting with the Lord over Abram's questions about his own future. God has already promised to make "a great nation" of Abram, but Abram is looking for more concrete assurance. Here is how God responds:

> *Then He brought him outside and said, "Look now toward heaven, and count the stars if you are able to number them." And He said to him, "So shall your descendants be." (Gen. 15:5 NKJV)*

We are then told that Abram believed God and that God "accounted it to him for righteousness" (Gen. 15:6 NKJV). This is a major reason for believing that having faith in God comes ahead of salvation: Even as early in the Bible as the story of Abraham, God was showing us that we cannot base a true relationship with Him on any other foundation than faith.

What made Abram unique was his willingness to extend his initial faith in God and actively trust in God, by both accepting and acting on what he was told. This will become even more clear—and dramatic—when we read of Abram's son, Isaac, in chapter 6.

Meanwhile, God willingly responded to Abram's honest questions, even when Abram asked how he could know for sure that God would keep His promise. At that point, the Lord initiated a blood covenant with Abram, similar to other ancient blood covenants that have been written about extensively by many authors. The main point to remember here is that a blood covenant is eternal.

Why do you think that God considered Abram such a righteous and faithful man?

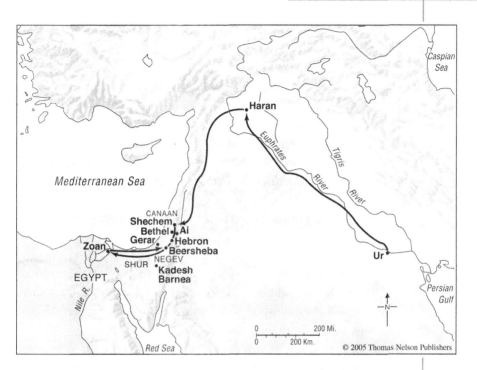

THE BIRTH OF ISHMAEL

The first 15 verses of chapter 16 then tell us how, despite his trust in the Lord, Abram and Sarai still got antsy and tried to make things happen on their own. (After all, he was already eighty-six years old and her age was surely comparable!) It was common practice in that era for a woman who was unable to have children of her own to do so through a surrogate. In Sarai's case that person was her handmaiden, Hagar, whom Sarai "gave" to Abram so that he could father a child.

But things never work out very well when we get ahead of God and try to do things for Him! In this case, as soon as Hagar became pregnant, she became insolent toward Sarai, whom she now considered her inferior. This resulted in so much discord between the two women that Hagar tried to flee, only to be sent back to Abram by an angel who told her:

47

"Behold, you are with child,
And you shall bear a son.
You shall call his name Ishmael,
Because the Lord has heard your affliction.
He shall be a wild man;
His hand shall be against every man,
And every man's hand against him.
And he shall dwell in the presence of all his
brethren." (Gen. 16:11–12 NKJV)

Today, the modern descendants of Ishmael are generally considered to be the Arab nations.

Chapter 17 tells how God instituted the rite of circumcision for Abram and all his descendants, as a sign of the covenant God had established with Abram. God also changed Abram's name to Abraham, and Sarai's to Sarah.

To those who study ancient covenants, this also signifies the giving of something of personal value to the other party, always a part of a blood covenant. According to that understanding, in this case God gave both Abraham and Sarah the "h" of His own name. In the ancient Hebrew language it was spelled without vowels as YHWH; modern transliterations sometime render it Yahweh. Either way, Abram and Sarai both received the same portion.

Chapter 18 features the familiar visit with Abraham of three men who are generally considered to have been the Lord Himself in human form, plus two angels. After Abraham served them a meal they reminded him that God had promised him a son of his own, at which Sarah—listening from the tent—could not keep from laughing! God then reinforced His promise, saying, "Is anything too hard for the LORD?" (Gen. 18:14 NKJV).

What "impossible promise" in your life has God fulfilled?

THE STORY OF ABRAHAM, PART THREE

SODOM AND GOMORRAH

We come next to the destruction of Sodom and Gomorrah, preceded by a fascinating interchange between Abraham and the Lord. Abraham was convinced that Sodom must contain at least a few righteous people, and so he bargained with God accordingly. Alas, not even ten could be found, and so the Lord did what He knew had to be done, sparing only Lot and his immediate family.

From what you know about the destruction of Sodom and Gomorrah, do you consider it fair? Was it necessary?

What happened to Lot's wife was tragic, but certainly illustrates how important it can be to do exactly what God tells us to do! Later, the story of Lot and his two daughters, who got him drunk and then slept with him in the cave, provides more fascinating insights into the Hebraic culture of that era. Children, as always, were highly valued, especially among women who saw their sons and daughters as potential caretakers for themselves in their old age. In this case, the eventual descendants of one of Lot's daughters became the Moabites; of the other, the Ammonites.

Now the focus returns to Abraham, who journeyed southward with Sarah to the land of Gerar, ruled by a king called Abimelech. As though to prove that old habits die hard,

ABOUT THOSE HUSBANDS . . .

To the ancient Hebrews, as soon as a man and woman became engaged they were considered legally married. At that point, if one died the other could inherit the deceased partner's property, even though they had never gone through the official marriage ceremony itself and never physically consummated their legal union.

We have a good example of this in the story of Lot and his two daughters, who were called "married" in the Scriptures but in modern terminology were only "engaged." The first clue comes when Lot told the crowd outside his door that neither of his two daughters had ever known a man. The second clue comes when we are told that Lot had to go "without" his own house to contact his sons-in-law in the morning, while his own daughters were still living under his own roof.

The third clue, admittedly much weaker than the first two but interesting nonetheless, comes later on when the two daughters plied Lot with wine and then lay with him, because there was "no man on earth to come in unto us." The likelihood that either one, or both, might have had children (or been pregnant) by then, if they had actually cohabited with their husbands when they lived in Sodom, is fairly high.

Abraham once again told his new neighbors that Sarah was his sister, to protect himself from harm in case anyone wished to take her for his wife. And once again, as happened so many years before, God intervened and literally prevented Abimelech from sleeping with Sarah, although he had every intention of doing so.

Abimelech obeyed God, but he was not the least bit happy with Abraham! Here is what Abraham told him by way of explanation, notable because it shows how close Abraham came to telling the truth about Sarah . . . and yet how far away at the same time:

Because I thought, surely the fear of God is not in this place; and they will kill me on account of my wife. But indeed she is truly my sister. She is the daughter of my father, but not the daughter of my mother; and she

*became my wife. And it came to pass, when God caused
me to wander from my father's house, that I said to her,
"This is your kindness that you should do for me: in
every place, wherever we go, say of me, He is my brother." (Gen. 20:11–13 NKJV)*

THE BIRTH OF ISAAC

Finally, in Abraham and Sarah's old age but in God's perfect
timing (indeed, Abraham was 100 years old!), their long-
promised son, Isaac, was born. Abraham had him circumcised
on the eighth day, as God had commanded, and then invited
everyone to a party a few months later when Isaac was weaned.

Meanwhile, Hagar and Sarah again began to have difficulties,
arising from jealousy over whose son and which mother
would find greater favor in Abraham's eyes. Sarah resolved the
problem in her own way, by insisting that Abraham send
Hagar and Ishmael away. And God agreed, telling Abraham
not to be distressed, for though Isaac was the promised son of
the covenant, Ishmael, too, would eventually give rise to a
great nation.

And this is exactly how it turned out—for who can doubt the
horrific animosity that exists to this day between the Jews and
the Arabs, the former descending through Abraham and Isaac
and the latter descending through Abraham and Ishmael?

*What are some ways in which the modern-day rivalry between
these direct descendants of Abraham's two sons, Isaac and
Ishmael, is evident?*

A Perfect Day for Circumcision

In case you're wondering why God specified (for sure to Moses in Leviticus 12:3, but probably also to Abraham) that male children should be circumcised eight days after their birth, this is the first day on which the blood of a newborn is fully capable of clotting. Without that vital ability, male babies could easily have bled to death, especially in the primitive conditions under which circumcision was carried out in Abraham's and Moses' day.

Chapter 21 ends with a covenant, established between Abraham and his one-time nemesis, Abimelech. Their agreement was essentially a peace treaty, brought about by Abimelech's respect for Abraham as a man of God, on whom the blessings of God had visibly fallen.

Pulling It All Together . . .

• The story of the Tower of Babel is one of the most fascinating in the Bible. It's a story of blind pride and fierce ambition, misdirected toward the impossible goal of equality with God. It resulted in a massive geographical dispersion of the people of that era, into what we, today, might call distinctly different "ethnic" groups speaking many different languages.

• In their time, Sodom and Gomorrah were the most evil cities on earth, and God finally chose to destroy them utterly. Abraham bargained on their behalf, but even God Himself could not find ten righteous people in Sodom. Abraham's nephew, Lot, plus his wife and two daughters, were allowed to escape, but Lot's wife disobeyed God, looked behind her at the wrong moment, and was turned instantly into a pillar of salt.

• God's sacred covenant with Abraham, in which God promised an eternal blessing on Abraham and all his descendants, came into being in stages but still remains in effect thousands of years later. God operates on His own timetable, so the son He promised Abraham did not arrive as soon as Abraham might have preferred. But eventually, Isaac was born to Sarah, to continue Abraham's legacy exactly as God intended.

FROM ISAAC TO JACOB

GENESIS 22:1–28:22

Before We Begin . . .

The story of the rivalry between Jacob and Esau has been told many times. Assuming you've heard it at least once, what impression were you given about the strengths and weaknesses of these two men?

Considering that the firstborn always had primary inheritance rights in biblical times, why do you think God might have allowed Jacob to be born second when He had obviously chosen him to continue the lineage of Abraham and Isaac?

THE STORY OF ABRAHAM, PART FOUR

Of all the stories in the Bible, one of the most wrenching certainly has to be Abraham's near-sacrifice of his beloved, long-awaited son, Isaac. It's all there in the first nineteen verses of chapter 22, how . . .

- God instructed Abraham to "give back" his son.
- Abraham arose early in the morning.
- He split wood and then saddled his donkey.
- He collected two young male servants to help on the journey.
- He gathered Isaac and set off to another of those places that God promised to show him when he got there.

All these things show Abraham at his best, a man whose trust in the Lord was so absolute that the Bible records not a single word of doubt or dissent, even though he'd waited for years for God to fulfill His promise of a son—the very son he was now being asked to sacrifice!

Even though the Bible does not record Abraham questioning God in this act, how do you suppose Abraham was feeling? Why do you think God would put him through that?

But the story does not end in tragedy. On the contrary—God was testing Abraham, even as He frequently tests us to see if we really do trust Him as we often say we do. And the final result? God stayed the hand of Abraham at the last possible moment and sent him to a nearby thicket, where he found a ram caught by its horns. Thus God provided the sacrifice He required, and Isaac was spared. God then reconfirmed His covenant with Abraham, and Abraham and Isaac headed for home.

About Those Mountains . . .

Genesis 22:14 tells us that Abraham called the place where he almost sacrificed Isaac "The-Lord-Will-Provide." In Hebrew the words were *Yahweh Yir'eh*. The writer further explains their meaning as "in the mount of the Lord it shall be provided." This concept connects, later on, with the way God called Moses to "come up the mountain" to talk to Him and receive His instructions. Likewise it comes into play in a number of recorded encounters with God—for example, Elijah and the prophets of Baal on Mount Carmel (1 Kings 18:20–40), or Christ, Moses, and Elijah on the Mount of Transfiguration in Matthew 17:1–3. And, of course, in modern times we often speak of "mountaintop experiences."

Why do you suppose God uses mountains to bring people closer when He wants to talk to them, but didn't like the Tower of Babel concept?

Chapter 22 ends with a short genealogy that might not seem significant, except for one thing. Abraham's brother, Nahor, had a son named Bethuel, who then had a daughter named Rebekah, whom we shall meet soon enough.

In chapter 23 we see graphic proof of how much Abraham cared for his beloved wife, Sarah. He mourned and wept for her when she passed away, but he also went out of his way to find an appropriate burial place where her body could be safe forever from any kind of violation.

ANCIENT HEBREW BURIALS

In Abraham's time, those who died were not always buried underground. Their bodies were bathed, rubbed in fragrant spices, and often put in a safe place, such as a cave, to allow the flesh to disappear via natural processes, leaving only the bones behind. As we mention in chapter 9 of this study guide, this is probably what happened to Joseph. Before he passed away in Egypt he ordered that his bones should one day be carried back to the land of Canaan, from whence he had come to Egypt so many years before.

What seems especially interesting here (and perhaps even endearing!) is the short series of negotiations undertaken by Abraham and the people of the land in which Sarah died. It simply was not customary to negotiate a thing like this in what we might call the rough, sometimes confrontational "western" manner. Rather, all those associated with the eventual seller of the property went to great lengths to appear totally disinterested in the proceedings. The seller even offered the land for nothing to Abraham, then named a "market" price but still said, "What is that [400 shekels] between you and me?" (Gen. 23:15 NKJV)

The paragraph above refers to ancient barter customs. Much of that part of the world still uses the same system, in which nothing that's for sale has a fixed price. Why do you think this custom did not become part of our Western heritage?

WHO WILL SELL ME SOME LAND?

We have already pointed out the unique way in which the people of Abraham's time sometimes negotiated for land. A similar example can be found in 2 Samuel 24:21–24, detailing David's negotiations for a threshing floor on which to build an altar to God, owned by a man named Araunah.

ISAAC AND REBEKAH

Now we find Abraham, approaching 140 years of age, attending to one last detail before he could consider his life complete: Isaac needs a wife! And so, in true patriarchal fashion, Abraham enlisted the aid of his most trusted servant, a man who is not named in this chapter but who can be identified as Eliezer, the same servant mentioned in Genesis 15:2–3 when Abraham was still yearning for a son of his own:

> *But Abram said, "Lord God, what will You give me, seeing I go childless, and the heir of my house is Eliezer of Damascus?" Then Abram said, "Look, You have given me no offspring; indeed one born in my house is my heir!" (NKJV)*

Abraham sent his servant back to the land of Abraham's own ancestry to choose a wife for Isaac. Why did he not send Isaac himself?

The remainder of chapter 24 then breaks down into a four-step process:

First, Abraham gave Eliezer his commission to return to the land in which Abraham's family still lived, to find a wife for Isaac among Abraham's own people.

Second, when he arrived in the land of Abraham's ancestry, Eliezer prayed and trusted the Lord to guide and direct what he was about to do.

Third, Eliezer negotiated with Rebekah's brother to win the hand of Rebekah for his master's son.

Fourth, Rebekah agreed to return with Eliezer to marry Isaac, who by then was forty years of age himself and was definitely ready. This, by the way, is how we know Abraham's age at the time, since he was 100 years old when Isaac was born.

The details of this story are as lovely as the overall contours—the giving of the nose rings (as common then as earrings are today) and bracelets, the gifts to the family—but most of all the instant willingness of Rebekah herself to go and do what was clearly the will of the Lord. Or maybe not so clear to those who were there at the time, but clear to us as we look backward.

WHAT KIND OF MAN WAS ISAAC?

The Bible does not tell us how Isaac felt or behaved during those moments on the sacrificial altar when it certainly looked bad for him. Tradition has it that he cooperated fully, without resistance, even though he undoubtedly knew what was coming. If so, God surely must have been part of that scenario.

It's also worth noting that Jewish historians believe Isaac was not a young boy at the time, but a fully grown man. They claim that Isaac was twenty years old or more (indeed, one commentator believes he was thirty-three years old, the same age as Christ when He gave His life centuries later—remember, God truly believes in symbolism), and thus would be very much aware of what almost happened to him. Still he appeared quite willing to cooperate fully, even carrying a heavy load of firewood (enough to consume a human body) up a mountain to what could have been his own death. Think about it—this is also something a young boy would not have had the physical strength to do.

Years later, the Scriptures tell us that Isaac had gone out to the field to meditate when he saw the caravan that brought Rebekah to him. These two insights into Isaac's character certainly suggest that he had a healthy relationship with God.

How did Rebekah's behavior toward Eliezer indicate her strength of character and her willingness to obey God?

The story comes to a graceful close when Isaac ". . . went out to meditate in the field in the evening; and he lifted his eyes and looked, and there, the camels were coming" (Gen. 24:63 NKJV). And on those camels, of course, was his future wife, whom he lodged in his mother's tent until they were married, undoubtedly within a very short time.

The first verses of chapter 25 give us final details from Abraham's life. After Sarah died he took a concubine named Keturah, who gave him a great number of sons during the last years of his life—when he was between 138 and 175 years old.

Then at last, "Abraham died in a good old age, an old man and full of years" (Gen. 25:8 NKJV) and was buried in the same cave he'd bought for Sarah almost forty years before. What's interesting here is that Isaac and Ishmael together buried their father. So, even though Abraham had long since sent Ishmael away, to make it clear that God's covenant through Abraham's descendants would pass through Isaac, Abraham and Sarah's own son, as God intended, Ishmael must have been close enough to be notified that his father's time had come. And, though we have no real evidence, it would at least seem that Ishmael and Isaac were able to get along well enough to cooperate in the burial of their father.

Where was Ishmael during all the years prior to the death of Abraham? How do you suppose he got back in time to assist with his father's funeral?

The last portion of chapter 25 shows us where the descendants of Ishmael and Isaac settled. Then we are given some of the details of the birth of Isaac and Rebekah's twin boys, Esau and Jacob.

JACOB AND ESAU

Few characters in the Bible (and certainly no sets of twins) have been written about as much as Jacob and Esau. Most commentators tend to portray Jacob as a weakling and a deceiver, and Esau as a man's man who preferred hunting wild game to hanging around the campfire and doing "women's work." Let us look a little more closely at some of these traditional views.

First, God Himself made it very clear to Rebekah that, even though Jacob would not be the firstborn, he would have primacy over Esau:

Two nations are in your womb, Two peoples shall be separated from your body; One people shall be stronger than the other, And the older shall serve the younger. (Gen. 25:23 NKJV)

Why God allowed Esau to be born first if He intended to continue Abraham's lineage through Jacob is a mystery that only God can resolve, but surely He had reasons we cannot know.

Second, the story of Jacob's trickery, by which he supposedly took advantage of Esau and stole Esau's birthright, contains cultural clues that are not always considered. For example, God had long since established what later became the nation of Israel as a nation of farmers and herders, who grew most of what they needed to survive in the ground and on the hoof. Hunting wild game for sport, as Esau liked to do, was not expressly forbidden, but it might have been considered a borderline occupation for anyone who expected to be the leader of the people. In other words, Esau was not automatically disqualified, but his primary interests certainly did not put him in the mainstream as an obvious "leader of God's people."

Third, "Why Was Jacob Cooking Stew?" elsewhere in this chapter talks a bit more about that subject, while we will see further evidence of Jacob's manliness in "Who Moved That Stone?" in the next chapter.

Fourth, as told in Genesis, chapter 27, the one action for which Jacob must certainly be held accountable was his deception of his own father, in which he disguised himself (with Rebekah's help) as his older brother and literally stole the blessing Isaac thought he was giving to Esau. In this, however, Jacob actually proved that he was a "chip off the old block." His own grandfather, Abraham, by cohabiting with Hagar and producing

WHAT'S IN A NAME?

The names of Esau and Jacob are fascinating studies in Hebrew wordplay. These ancient people, often with God's help, did their best to name their sons and daughters very carefully, according to who the children seemed to be. Thus Esau's name ties in directly with his "redness" (perhaps in both his skin tones and his hair) and his general hairiness. Jacob's name, usually transliterated into English as *Ya'akov* (but translated as Jacob), has several possible meanings, as do many Hebrew words. The one most commonly associated with him would be "heel-catcher," since he came from the womb literally grasping his brother's heel.

Ishmael, also ran ahead of God and tried to make things happen that the Lord, in His own timing, clearly intended to bring about in His own way. But of course, now we'll never know what God's original plan for Jacob would have entailed!

Why do you think God chose Jacob to perpetuate the blessings God had promised to Abraham and his descendants?

THE STOLEN BLESSING

Chapter 26 tells us a fascinating tale about Isaac, Rebekah, and a king named Abimelech. Isaac did almost exactly the same thing that Abraham had done to an earlier king of the same name. He visited the king's land during a famine, feared for his own life if the people of that place knew he was married to such a beautiful woman (in this case Rebekah rather than Sarah), and thus tried to pass her off as his sister rather than his wife. The eventual result was a covenant between the current Abimelech and Isaac, but not without some needless wrangling that did not exactly "do Isaac proud."

WHY WAS JACOB COOKING STEW?

In ancient Hebrew camps it was the job of the firstborn son to maintain a common cooking pot for the benefit of anyone who needed food. Thus the stew that Jacob was tending when Esau came back from hunting; for Esau preferred to hunt rather than to fulfill his responsibility as the firstborn son. In this and probably other ways as well, Jacob had already taken Esau's place, even before the birthright sale. Even so, some commentators have mistakenly called Jacob a sissy or even a "mama's boy," literally for honoring the customs of his people and assuming a responsibility his older brother had shunned—and perhaps even disdained.

Why do you suppose Isaac did exactly as Abraham had done? Is it possible that Abraham passed along his own "war stories" to his son?

What do you know about ancient society that would help explain why Abraham and Isaac both felt it necessary to practice this particular deceit?

Finally, after some discussion of Isaac's arguments and negotiations over water rights with his neighbors (an age-old problem that was also common to the American West during the nineteenth and early twentieth centuries), we come to another of those biblical scenes that have almost become common folklore. That scene, of course, is the one we have already mentioned, the deception of Isaac into giving his blessing to Jacob instead of Esau.

There is no question that Rebekah and Jacob pulled a fast one on Isaac, who was done in by three things: (1) his failing eyesight, (2) his taste for wild game, and (3) Rebekah's overhearing his conversation with Esau, at which point she knew instantly what she had to do to swing events in Jacob's direction. All the details are right there in chapter 27—Jacob's fear that their deception would not work, his wearing of Esau's best clothes, and his mother's use of goatskins to fool his father's probing fingers.

How do you think Rebekah fastened the goatskins to Jacob's arms?

WHY WAS THE FATHER'S BLESSING SUCH A BIG DEAL?

In the modern world we tend to forget how important a father's blessing was to his children in ancient times. In a word it was everything; in the case of Esau and Jacob it literally defined who would prosper and who would live a more difficult life. Furthermore, the custom of passing the blessing (and the main inheritance) on to the firstborn son has not disappeared entirely. Among many examples of the laws and customs of inheritance, even as this study guide goes to press, an anxious United Kingdom waits for the day when Queen Elizabeth will pass her crown to her oldest son, now a prince but then to become King Charles.

(And by the way, despite what many people have thought over the years, Rebekah did not use sheepskins. The wool on a sheep might have been a dead giveaway—it's far more thick and luxurious and unlike human hair than the hair on a goat!) The inevitable result of all this chicanery was an angry Esau, enraged over the loss of both his birthright and his blessing to his younger brother. Truly, Jacob feared for his life, so once more Rebekah stepped in. She convinced Isaac that Jacob needed to take a wife from her own people rather than their neighbors, at which point Isaac called Jacob in and sent him off to visit his uncle Laban.

Note that this is the exact opposite of what happened in Isaac's own case. Abraham sent a servant while Isaac (the son) stayed home and waited; Isaac sent his son instead. Just as Rebekah had heard of Esau's monumental discontent, Isaac was probably also aware of what might yet happen between the two brothers and was therefore willing to send Jacob away—if only to save his life!

Which would you prefer—to pick your own wife/husband, or to have a servant do it for you?

Thus Jacob went on his way while Esau stayed home and married Mahalath, the daughter of Isaac's half-brother Ishmael and thus his half-cousin.

A LADDER TO THE SKY

On his way to his uncle Laban's home, Jacob stopped for the night, used a stone for a pillow, and promptly dreamed of a ladder ascending to heaven, with angels climbing up and down.

This particular dream has been interpreted any number of ways, but surely it indicated at least two significant things:

First, God Himself appeared to Jacob in the dream and confirmed that the covenant He had established with Abraham and Isaac would now be extended through Jacob. Obviously God was faithful even though Jacob had tried to take things into his own hands and had not exactly been righteous in all that he'd done!

Second, Jacob, by his actions from that point forward, responded to God's assurance in a most positive way. Perhaps his narrow escape from Esau's wrath, coupled with chagrin over the deception he'd already been part of, was beginning to humble him and make him realize how much he already owed to the Lord's infinite patience. Here is what he said:

> Then Jacob made a vow, saying, "If God will be with me, and keep me in this way that I am going, and give me bread to eat and clothing to put on, so that I come back to my father's house in peace, then the Lord shall be my God. And this stone which I have set as a pillar shall be God's house, and of all that You give me I will surely give a tenth to You." (Gen. 28:20–22 NKJV)

If you have heard or read of the "Jacob's Ladder" dream before, how have you interpreted it?

PULLING IT ALL TOGETHER . . .

• Abraham almost made the ultimate sacrifice of his own son, Isaac. But God had merely been testing him, and once again Abraham proved that he trusted God above all else.

• When Isaac came of age, Abraham sent his servant to find Isaac a wife from his own people. Many things had to go right on that trip, but God worked things out perfectly to bring Isaac and Rebekah together and make them instant sweethearts.

• Jacob and Esau were twins, with Esau first but Jacob holding on to his heel as they were born. This turned out to be a prophetic image, with Jacob effectively taking Esau's place as the "son of the blessing," proclaimed first by God and second by Isaac himself—though Isaac most assuredly was not 100 percent aware of who he was blessing!

• By the end of Genesis 28, Jacob was well on his way to deserving (as much as any of us ever are!) the blessings that God had long since determined to pour out upon him and his descendants.

6   THE TWELVE SONS OF JACOB

GENESIS 29:1–35:29

Before We Begin . . .

How many of the twelve sons of Jacob can you name, without reading this chapter (or Genesis 35) first? Who was the first? The last? The next-to-last, and also the most well-known?

The vision that came to Jacob in the place he called Bethel, of the ladder reaching into heaven with the angels climbing up and down, marked a turning point in Jacob's life. The covenant between God and his father, Abraham, then became equally real to Jacob, and very much his covenant, as well. God showed Jacob that He would preserve and protect him, just as He had done for Abraham and Isaac before him. Jacob then responded as shown at the end of the previous chapter, by vowing faithfulness and building a monument to God, using the stone he'd rested his head on the night before.

Now Jacob turned his eyes toward the future and traveled onward, to the home of his uncle Laban. We met Laban earlier when he bargained with Abraham's servant for a wife (Laban's sister, Rebekah) for Jacob's father, Isaac. When Jacob arrived in the general vicinity he stopped at a well, talked to some of the local herdsmen, and found that he was in the right place.

Almost immediately, God brought Laban's lovely daughter, Rachel, to the well to water her sheep, and Jacob found himself instantly smitten. Like her aunt Rebekah before her—and Abraham's wife, Sarah, as well—Rachel was another extremely beautiful woman. Jacob did the manly thing, wrestled the cover off the well all by himself, watered her sheep, identified himself, and then kissed her (but as a relative only) and wept. He was glad to be there.

In what ways do you already see God's covenant with Abraham extending to his grandson Jacob?

WHO MOVED THAT STONE?

In Genesis 29:10 we are told that Jacob rolled a large stone from the well to which Rachel had come with her sheep. Such a well stone was normally handled by several men at once, as detailed previously. Clearly, if Jacob were the physical weakling he has sometimes been called, he could not have managed this physical feat by himself.

Then came what many people consider one of the most shameless deceptions in the Bible. Jacob agreed to work seven years for Laban, in return for the right to marry Rachel. But when their wedding night came, Laban substituted his older daughter, Leah, who apparently was not especially attractive (although the Bible tells us only that she had "weak eyes"), and Jacob had no way of knowing that he'd been deceived until the morning.

Is it conceivable to you that Jacob could be so utterly fooled? What factors, cultural and otherwise, might have worked for and against such a deception?

Jacob then confronted Laban, who justified his deception by explaining that it simply was not proper to marry off the younger daughter before the older. But would Jacob like to work another seven years for Rachel? Jacob agreed, gave Leah her full seven-day "bridal week" (which, by tradition, involved a lot of feasting and a lot of "alone time" for the new couple), and was then given Rachel for his second wife.

At that point Jacob was committed to another seven years of servitude to Laban, even though Rachel was already "his" in a very real sense. The Bible tells us that the first seven years "seemed only a few days to him." It says nothing of the second seven years, but given the conflicts he eventually got into with Laban, over ownership of the flocks and herds that prospered so mightily under his direction, they were probably not peaceful years by comparison.

If you have heard this story before, was it your impression that Jacob and Rachel became man and wife before or after Jacob worked the second seven years? Read the passage carefully again. What, specifically, does the Bible say about the timeline of events?

What are the lessons of all this? Consider the following:

First, though the Lord extended the covenant to Jacob and re-verified all His promises to Abraham, that didn't mean that Jacob would get off scot-free for his own deception of Isaac and Esau. This was payback time, and Jacob knew it.

Second, in a larger sense, Jacob's experience with Laban and his two daughters illustrated the principle that what a man sows, he also reaps.

Third, if you track all the nuances, you will see remarkable parallels between Jacob's treatment of his own brother and Laban's treatment of Jacob. The brazen substitution of one person for another, the stealing of another's rightful future, the bold lies and false implications—these are not coincidences at all, but impossible-to-miss correlations that only God could orchestrate.

The remainder of Genesis 29, and much of chapter 30 as well, detail the births of Jacob's sons. The rivalry between Leah and Rachel is interesting and even amusing sometimes—note the story of the mandrakes, commonly thought to be aphrodisiacs, in Genesis 30:14–16.

But that's not what matters most here. The twelve young men born to Jacob's two wives and their two handmaidens will all play important parts, both as individuals and as a group, in the stories that follow. These sons are the ones who eventually gave rise to the twelve tribes of Israel.

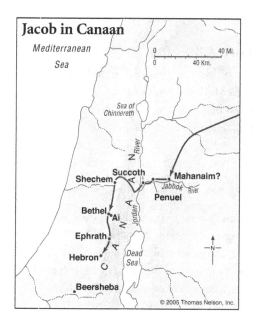

Jacob in Canaan

© 2005 Thomas Nelson, Inc.

JACOB'S TROUBLES WITH LABAN

By the time all twelve of his sons had been born, Jacob was ready to go back to his own land. But Laban had other ideas:

> . . . *for I have learned by experience that the Lord has blessed me for your sake." Then he said, "Name me your wages, and I will give it." (Gen. 30:27–28 NKJV)*

Jacob was more interested in building up his own wealth, so he worked out what we might call an "entrepreneurial deal" with Laban. By the terms they agreed on, Jacob appeared to be taking all the risks, yet he still managed to dramatically increase his own flocks even more than Laban's. The means by which he did this are not easy to understand. They also involve considerable back-and-forth wordplay in the original Hebrew, which makes what he did all the more fascinating but no easier to explain.

esu WHEN DOES A WARNING BECOME A BLESSING?

The "Mizpah," commonly known as a "blessing" between friends (and often inscribed on coins), is based on Genesis 31:48–50, which says:

And Laban said, "This heap is a witness between you and me this day." Therefore its name was called Galeed, also Mizpah, because he said, *"May the Lord watch between you and me when we are absent one from another.* If you afflict my daughters, or if you take other wives besides my daughters, although no man is with us—see, God is witness between you and me!" (NKJV, italics added)

The italicized portion is often extracted as the "blessing" portion of the above Scripture. However, as most biblical scholars agree, context is everything! In the context of the verses in which it appears, the "Mizpah" is not a blessing at all. More accurately, it might be called a warning from Laban to Jacob, to the effect that Jacob had better be careful and not commit any more sins, because God would be watching!

Reread the story of Jacob's "methods" of increasing his own flock while not increasing Laban's. Then answer two questions: 1) Do you understand it? and 2) Was it fair?

However, the bottom line was much simpler to comprehend. God stepped in and multiplied Jacob's wealth, in spite of (and probably not because of) all of Jacob's peeled-stick manipulations.

JACOB FLEES

Two things finally pushed Jacob to "make the break" from Laban and return to the land of his birth:

1. He had an overwhelming sense that it was time to go back home and face his brother.

2. He recognized growing unrest among the sons of Laban, who were beginning to suspect that Jacob was somehow cheating their father, even though the increase in Jacob's holdings was coming from God.

By what he saw on Laban's face, Jacob also realized that Laban's sons were turning him against Jacob. So Jacob called his wives out to the field and told them what he intended to do, and they were both ready to go. Next morning Jacob rounded up his animals, loaded all his household goods, put Leah and Rachel on camels, and headed back toward Canaan.

Why do you think Jacob called his wives out to the field to talk to them about leaving their father?

Three days later Laban learned what Jacob had done, and seven days after that he caught up with Jacob in the mountains. Then followed a spirited argument, for Laban was angry to see his daughters and grandchildren taken away without his approval, and Jacob was defensive even though he felt he had plenty of reasons to steal away in secret.

To make things worse, Rachel had stolen Laban's household gods. Clearly, she was either at least partially pagan, or she wished to do her father as much mental harm as she could. Either way, she managed to hide her deception by literally sitting on his gods (undoubtedly stone or wooden carvings) and insisting that she could not stand up at that time of the month.

The eventual result was a treaty, proposed by Laban, that allowed each man to save face by agreeing never to cross a certain line in the other's direction again. And at last Jacob, all his servants, all his wealth, all his wives and concubines, and all his children were on the road for good.

TOGETHER AGAIN

The major problem came when Jacob and his people got close enough to Canaan for Esau to realize that Jacob was coming back. What would he do? Would he still want revenge? This was certainly on Jacob's mind when messengers from Esau arrived, advising him that his brother was coming to meet him with four hundred men!

Like any good general, Jacob immediately divided his entire entourage into two traveling companies, vowing that if Esau attacked one, the other would still have a chance to escape. Later that night, before settling down, he pulled out a huge number of goats, sheep, camels, cows, bulls, and donkeys, instructing his herders to drive them ahead of everyone else as a present (a peace offering) for Esau.

How do you think Jacob was feeling as he journeyed to the land of his birth and prepared to meet Esau again?

FEAST OF SUCCOTH

In Genesis 33:17, after Jacob returned to his homeland, he bought some acreage and built a house for himself and booths for his livestock. Later on, God commanded the children of Israel to observe His seven holy feast days (also called festivals) in Leviticus 23:33–44. He called this the Feast of Tabernacles, which is more commonly called the "Feast of Succoth." Surely it cannot be coincidence that Jacob himself, when he returned to his ancestral home, built succoth (i.e., booths) in a place called Succoth. God is into symbolism in a big way!

When darkness fell that evening, as happened many years before, Jacob had another encounter with God that marked another major change in his life. This time he wrestled for the entire night with a stranger, whom he somehow seemed to know was God Himself. Again we see the physical strength of Jacob, for he refused to let the stranger go and contended with him until daybreak, even when his own hip had been forced out of joint, leaving him with a permanent limp. He finally released the stranger only when he blessed Jacob and gave him another name, as recorded in Genesis 32:28–29:

> And He said, "Your name shall no longer be called Jacob, but Israel; for you have struggled with God and with men, and have prevailed." Then Jacob asked, saying, "Tell me Your name, I pray." And He said, "Why is it that you ask about My name?" And He blessed him there. (NKJV)

By this act God bestowed on Jacob the name that has since been carried forward for thousands of years. Jacob's descendants have been called "the children of Israel," "the Nation of Israel," or just "Israel" alone in countless biblical and secular references from that point forward.

In the passage above, God gave Jacob a new name—just as He had changed the name of Jacob's grandfather, Abraham. Why do you think God chose to change these men's names? What would be the significance of such an act?

Can you imagine physically wrestling with God? Why do you think God chose to approach Jacob in this way?

The first seventeen verses of chapter 33 then give us a lesson in forgiveness and reconciliation. Despite all of Jacob's fears and protective measures, Esau had long since forgiven him.

When the two finally met, he fell on his neck with kisses and hugs. Esau didn't even want the gifts Jacob offered, but Jacob insisted, and soon the two men were living in peace in the same country again.

SHAME AND RETRIBUTION

Genesis 34 tells us the story of Dinah, one of Jacob's daughters, who went to visit some of the Canaanite women near her new home. But she was abducted and raped by a Canaanite man named Shechem. Shechem's father tried to calm things down by offering to make a marriage at any bride price Jacob might name, and Dinah's brothers seemed to agree.

But Dinah's brothers had other plans; they then pulled off a deception that seems more than a little harsh from these many years removed. Nonetheless it was actually a rigid enforcement of God's prohibition against intermarriage with the pagan Canaanites. First, Dinah's brothers dangled the possibility of a covenant of peace with the men of Shechem's city, if they would all consent to circumcision. Then, when the

WHY THE TRIBE OF LEVI?

Some have suggested that God was engaging in a bit of irony, hundreds of years later, when He assigned all the priestly functions to the tribe of Levi, which is the tribe that both Moses and his brother Aaron came from. While the children of Israel were encamped in the wilderness, after God brought them out of Egypt but before He brought them into the Promised Land, the sons of Aaron were made responsible for slaughtering all the sacrificial animals, sprinkling the blood on the altar, and performing all the other duties of the priests.

The "irony concept" suggests that God was saying to the sons of Levi, as a result of what Levi himself did in chapter 34 of Genesis: "Hey! You want to shed blood, I'll give you blood!" This cannot be proven for no one knows the mind of God, but certainly He does not forget—and certainly He does like to promote a certain sense of order and justice that we cannot always comprehend.

men agreed, thinking that a covenant with all these wealthy strangers would be a good thing (after all, intermarriage is a two-way street), Dinah's two most passionate brothers, Simeon and Levi, waited until their rivals were in maximum pain from their circumcisions, then fell upon them and killed every last man with swords.

Jacob was not pleased with what his sons had done, but he could not really counter their response in Genesis 34:31: "Should he treat our sister like a harlot?" (NKJV) Thus God sometimes uses the most unlikely people—and even what we might consider harsh means—to bring about obedience to His commands.

ONE MORE BLESSING

God begins chapter 35 by reminding Jacob of the vow he'd made many years before, on his way to Laban's house, when he dreamed the ladder dream at the place he called Bethel. Jacob then did what he should have done previously—he got rid of all the pagan gods in his household and required everyone to purify themselves and put on fresh clothes.

When they arrived at Bethel, Jacob built an altar, at which point God once again renewed His covenant with Jacob and all his descendants. This time He made it even clearer than before that Jacob was to be called Israel from then on, as he was in the verses that followed.

Three more things happened before the chapter ended:

1. Rachel died in childbirth and was buried nearby. But her newborn son, Benjamin, survived and became the last of the twelve.

2. Jacob's twelve sons, with the names of their mothers, were all listed in Genesis 35:23–26, as follows:

The sons of Leah were Reuben, Jacob's firstborn, and Simeon, Levi, Judah, Issachar, and Zebulun; the sons of Rachel were Joseph and Benjamin; the sons of Bilhah, Rachel's maidservant, were Dan and Naphtali; and the sons of Zilpah, Leah's maidservant, were Gad and Asher. (NKJV)

This is a list worth remembering, although it is not given here in chronological order.

3. The chapter ends with the death of Isaac, Jacob's father, at the age of 180 years.

PULLING IT ALL TOGETHER ...

• Jacob's meeting of Rachel at the well provides a lovely picture of love at first sight between a man and a woman.

• What Laban did to Jacob, with respect to Leah and Rachel, was inexcusable. And yet, from that deception God brought forth the twelve sons of Jacob, who later became the twelve tribes of Israel. Jacob outmaneuvered Laban in the end, both by how he increased his own wealth and how he got out from under Laban's control with all his family and his possessions intact. Surely God was in the middle of all this!

• Jacob's reunion with Esau could have been disastrous. Indeed, Jacob tried to prepare for every possibility. But again God had other plans, and therefore things went off without a hitch.

• The story of what happened to Jacob's daughter, Dinah—and what Jacob's own sons did in return—is difficult to read without shuddering. Certainly there was sin on one side, but was there also some overreaction on the other?

7

JOSEPH GOES TO EGYPT

GENESIS 36:1–38:30

Before We Begin ...

What has been your impression of Joseph as a young man, based on the familiar "coat of many colors" story? Was he wise for his age, unwise, or about right?

How does Joseph's brothers' hatred of him strike you? Does it seem excessive? How could it be strong enough to make them want to kill him?

In typical Hebraic fashion, chapter 36 of Genesis concludes the genealogy of one complete generation before moving on to the next. In this case, it lists the sons and grandsons of Esau, Jacob's brother, whose descendants became the Edomites. We will meet them many times more in other parts of the Bible, for they were often at war with the Israelites, just as the two brothers who gave them life were sometimes at war, as well.

However, this chapter is not so easy to follow, because the names of some of Esau's wives do not match some of the references in earlier chapters, either because Esau married additional women or because one or two of his previous wives were renamed somewhere along the way. As we have already seen, this was not a completely uncommon practice in that era—men and women "were" their names, and sometimes these were changed to bring them into better harmony with a person's changing personality.

Do we still think that people sometimes "are their names" today? Do you get mental images when you hear certain names? Can you give any examples?

The main point to remember from this genealogy is the difference between Jacob/Israel and Esau in terms of who and how they married. God chose to extend His covenant with Abraham and Isaac through Jacob, who then did as God desired by choosing a wife from among his own people—literally, the daughter of his mother's brother, or his own cousin. (Or, perhaps we should say daughters because he wound up with both Rachel and Leah!)

Esau did exactly the opposite, choosing several wives from the Canaanites, well-known for their pagan ways. Sadly, this illustrates a theme we will see recurring many times throughout the history of the children of Israel. God knew them well, and knew that pagan wives would pull them away from Him. At the same time, He was (and is) a jealous God, and made it very clear that He would not allow them to worship other gods in His place. Esau was among the first to do this, and it's hard to escape the conclusion that he did so in anger and defiance after his brother took both his birthright and his paternal blessing.

We will never know how all of this might have worked out if God had been allowed to handle it in His own way.

THE STORY OF JOSEPH

Many people consider the story of Joseph one of the most fascinating, informative, and inspiring in the Bible. Certainly it is among the most familiar—the famous "coat of many colors" story has been told and retold thousands of times. It even became the basis of a Broadway play several years ago.

Joseph's story begins in chapter 37 and extends all the way through the final fourteen chapters of Genesis, with the exception of one chapter that we will discuss momentarily. Verses 3 and 4 of chapter 37 help introduce Joseph and tell us almost everything we need to know to understand what follows:

Now Israel loved Joseph more than all his children, because he was the son of his old age. Also he made him a tunic of many colors. But when his brothers saw that their father loved him more than all his brothers, they hated him and could not speak peaceably to him. (Gen. 37:3–4 NKJV)

THE COAT OF MANY COLORS

For hundreds of years, the coat given by Jacob to his favorite son, Joseph, has been called a "coat of many colors." However, the correct translation of the original Hebrew words (*k'thonet passin*) was "royal robe." But what was a "royal robe" to the people of Joseph's time?

Most adult Hebrew men of that era, who worked in the fields or did any other kind of physical labor, wore robes with shortened sleeves that left their hands and lower arms free. The same robes were also somewhat shorter in overall length, so the wearer could bend over and do other kinds of work without constantly dragging his garments on the ground.

However, the "royal robe" given by Jacob to Joseph was the kind that might be worn by an older man who no longer worked the fields, a young man who was not yet old enough for regular labor, or a nobleman who had no need to do physical work. These robes completely covered the arms and came down low to the ankles, to protect the wearer from the sun.

Unfortunately, when the King James translators—working from a Greek translation of the original Hebrew called the Septuagint—came to this passage they had no apparent understanding of what the words actually meant, and thus translated the passage according to the standards of seventeenth-century English society, in which the nobility often wore clothes of many brilliant colors.

Beyond that, the people of Joseph's time had limited means by which to dye their clothes. Most fabrics were left to their natural colors.

In truth, Joseph was not the only son of Jacob's old age. He shared that distinction with Benjamin, for Joseph was son number eleven and Benjamin was number twelve. Perhaps more important, these two boys were the only sons of Rachel, the true love of Jacob's life, and Jacob undoubtedly had trouble concealing his strong feelings for both of them. In addition, Rachel died while giving birth to Benjamin, which is something else to remember, as later it becomes apparent that Jacob also loved Benjamin in a special way. Benjamin and Joseph were Jacob's last links to his beloved wife, and very well might have reminded him of her in many ways.

On the other hand, when he was still an immature seventeen-year-old youth, Joseph made the questionable decision to tell his brothers about two dreams he'd had. In the first dream, his brothers all bowed down to him; in the second dream, the sun, the moon, and eleven stars bowed down to him.

Why do you think Joseph was so willing to tell his brothers of his dreams—those dreams in which they served him? Was this wise, given how they already felt toward him as the "favored son" of Jacob?

Both dreams increased his brothers' loathing for Joseph and helped set the stage for what happened next:

1. Jacob sent Joseph out to a distant field to see how his brothers were doing. When they saw him coming, their hatred overwhelmed them and they plotted to kill him. Only his brother Reuben had pity on him, but even so, the best Reuben could do was to prevent the others from killing Joseph before they threw him into a deep pit. Reuben intended to sneak back later and rescue Joseph, but that's not how it worked out.

2. Instead, soon after the brothers put Joseph in the pit, a band of Midianite traders passed by, on their way to Egypt, and the brothers sold Joseph as a slave. Ironically, the Midianites were "sons of Ishmael," Joseph's grandfather's brother, whose descendants were already functioning—knowingly or otherwise—in opposition to God's chosen people.

3. On one hand, some would say that the traders saved Joseph's life, but others would say that God used them for His own purposes. Either way, Joseph soon found himself in Egypt, working for a man named Potiphar, one of the Pharaoh's officers and captain of the guard.

4. Meanwhile, Reuben returned to rescue Joseph and take him home to his father, but he came too late. The other brothers then took Joseph's tunic, dipped it in sheep's blood, gave it to their father, Jacob, and let him draw his own conclusions.

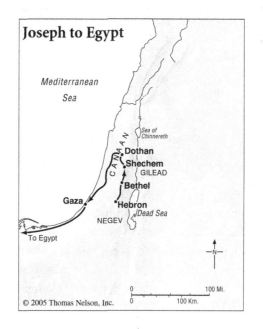

Joseph to Egypt

Mediterranean Sea

Sea of Chinnereth

CANAAN

Dothan

Shechem

GILEAD

Bethel

Gaza

Hebron

Dead Sea

NEGEV

To Egypt

—N—

0   100 Mi.
0   100 Km.

© 2005 Thomas Nelson, Inc.

JUDAH AND TAMAR

Chapter 38 of Genesis now "goes sideways" for a bit and tells us the story of Judah and Tamar. Judah was one of Jacob's sons by his first wife, Leah—the one who was substituted for Rachel. The Scriptures tell us that Judah "departed from his brothers" and visited some friends among the Canaanites. He then became infatuated with a certain Canaanite woman, married her (again, in direct opposition to what God had commanded His people), and soon had three sons—Er, Onan, and Shelah.

When Er came of age, Judah then selected a wife for him, a woman named Tamar. We are told nothing of Tamar's ancestry, but chances are she was an Israelite for she certainly knew one of the most important customs of the Israelites!

Those customs involved what were known as the "kinsman redeemer" laws, or the "Levirite Law" (based on the Latin word *levir,* meaning "husband's brother"). These laws, later codified by Moses in the book of Deuteronomy, were intended to protect Israelite widows in their old age by guaranteeing to them a fair opportunity to have legitimate sons and daughters to care for them, even if their husbands died before they had any children. In that situation, the oldest brother of the widow's husband was obligated to marry her even if he already had a wife, so she could have children.

Then, if the widow did have a son by her husband's brother, in legal terms that son would be considered the son of her original husband and would thus have all the corresponding inheritance rights to the widow's dead husband's property. Also, if the first "substitute husband" died without fathering any children, the second-oldest brother would then be obligated to perform the same duties, and so on down the line.

(This law forms the basis, incidentally, of the familiar passage in Matthew in which the Sadducees attempted to trip Jesus up by postulating a succession of seven brother-husbands for one widow, none of whom produced children. The question they thought so clever, in Matthew 22:28, was, ". . . in the resurrection, whose wife of the seven will she be?" (NKJV) Jesus, of course, had no trouble dispensing with this nonsense . . . but you'll have to look it up to get the answer!)

In Tamar's case, her first husband, Er, was so wicked he was killed by God, without producing children. Her second husband, Onan, used her for his own gratification but made sure he did not impregnate her, thus avoiding responsibility for raising her children. At that point, Tamar's third potential husband, Shelah, was too young for marriage. But even when he grew older, Judah refused to give him to her . . . and so she was stuck.

How Many Tamars in the Bible?

The story of Tamar and Judah is unique, but Tamar's name appears one other time in the Bible. Many years later, King David had a daughter named Tamar, full sister of a son named Absalom and half-sister to another son named Amnon. Sadly, both Tamars were violated by men who were related to them either by blood or marriage but were not their husbands. In the case of the first Tamar, things ended well even though Judah himself was certainly humbled. But as explained elsewhere in this chapter, what Tamar did to him was honorable within the context of the kinsman redeemer laws of that era—which were also invoked by Ruth and Boaz later on, by the way.

The second Tamar, as we are told in the book of 2 Samuel, was unable to do anything about her situation and suffered quite a bit as a result. But beyond that, her unfortunate rape by Amnon eventually brought about an horrific blood feud within her family, which ended in great sorrow for her father, David.

How does the killing of Er by God strike you? Does it seem fair? Why would God do such a thing? And why does He not seem to do similar things today?

This explains the elaborate deception she undertook, in which she disguised herself as a harlot, waited for Judah, her father-in-law, to come along, then enticed him into a dalliance that produced what she so desperately needed. In fact, she got two sons rather than one, whom she then named Perez and Zerah.

Meanwhile, she was also smart enough to keep Judah's signet, cord, and staff, supposedly as a security deposit against delivery of the goat Judah promised her for her services. Later on, by the time he sent the goat, the harlot he'd lain with could not be found. Thus Tamar still had the proof she needed when she later showed up pregnant and was accused of harlotry, for which Judah himself pronounced the customary sentence of death.

How ironic the situation, then, when she made her case, and how true his final words on the subject: "She has been more righteous than I, because I did not give her to Shelah my son" (Gen. 38:26 NKJV).

Why was what Tamar did considered honorable in the larger context? Does this story seem strange to you? In what ways?

PULLING IT ALL TOGETHER . . .

• Joseph was the eleventh son of Jacob. He and his younger brother, Benjamin, were the only sons of Rachel, the true love of Jacob's life. No wonder, then, that Jacob showed favoritism toward Joseph!

• Joseph told his older brothers of two dreams in which they bowed down to him. Combined with the jealousy they already felt, this pushed them over the edge and sent Joseph into slavery in Egypt.

• Tamar, daughter-in-law of Judah, wanted justice but couldn't get it via the normal route. So she took matters into her own hands and got the sons she knew she deserved, through her father-in-law, Judah.

8

JOSEPH SAVES THE NATION OF ISRAEL

GENESIS 39:1–50:26

Before We Begin . . .

What role did dreams play in the story of Joseph?

Why do you think God used dreams, and not direct conversation?

The last twelve chapters of Genesis tell the rest of the story of Joseph and his brothers. But they also give us a wondrous glimpse into how God provides for His own people. Jacob and his sons were close to perishing in a devastating famine that hit a few years after Joseph—as far as they knew—had "died."

But Joseph, of course, was not dead; he had simply gone ahead of them into a high leadership position in Egypt, from which he would save the children of Israel when the right time came. As always, God was fully able to preserve His chosen people for another day.

JOSEPH GOES TO PRISON

To review, Joseph was brought to Egypt by the Midianite traders who bought him from his brothers. He was then sold to the captain of Pharaoh's guard, a man named Potiphar. Before long, Joseph proved himself to be a very able manager and became overseer of Potiphar's house.

But Potiphar's wife (whose name we are not told) had other plans. One day she tried to entice Joseph into her bed, but he refused in the third-most-memorable line (the two best lines came later) of his story: "How then can I do this great wickedness, and sin against God?" (Gen. 39:9 NKJV)

Why did Joseph feel that lying with Potiphar's wife would be sinning against God rather than sinning against Potiphar? After all, the Ten Commandments hadn't been given yet (i.e., "You shall not commit adultery").

Unfortunately, Potiphar's wife didn't see things that way. Joseph escaped, but she held onto his garment (presumably his robe; this is also the second time Joseph's clothing was used against him!) and used that to turn the tables and convince her husband that Joseph had made an unwanted advance against her.

Joseph went immediately to prison, but even there God was with him. In a short time, Joseph's talents advanced him to the highest position of authority within the prison itself. At that point his position was probably equivalent to what we might call a "trusty" today, which refers to a convict so trustworthy he gets special privileges.

Given what you already know about Joseph, what talents did he obviously have at this point? How do you think he developed them?

Before long, Joseph was joined by two additional prisoners who came directly from the king of Egypt's palace—Pharaoh's butler and his baker. A few nights later, both prisoners had dreams that neither one could interpret, so they told them to Joseph. God gave him the interpretations, both of which turned out to be correct. As Joseph told them would happen, both men were taken back to Pharaoh's palace where the baker was hanged. Meanwhile, the butler regained his position but forgot about Joseph, even though Joseph had asked him to put in a good word with Pharaoh on his behalf.

Why do you think God gave dreams to Pharaoh's butler and baker? What was His real point in doing this?

Why do you think Pharaoh hanged the baker and spared the butler? Did God have anything to do with this?

JOSEPH'S RISE TO POWER

God again intervened a full two years later, when Pharaoh had two dreams in one night that none of the magicians and wise men in all of Egypt could figure out. At that point, his butler finally remembered Joseph, and Pharaoh immediately brought Joseph from the prison to see if he could help.

Pharaoh then told both of his dreams to Joseph, who explained that God alone could interpret Pharaoh's dreams, but that God would show Joseph what they meant. The first dream involved seven lean cows that devoured seven fat cows; the second dream involved seven withered heads of grain that devoured seven healthy heads.

Joseph explained that the seven fat cows and healthy heads of grain represented seven years of plenty, while the seven lean cows and withered heads of grain represented seven years of famine that would follow right behind. He then recommended storing a portion of all the produce of the land, under Pharaoh's authority, during the years of plenty so they'd have food during the seven years of famine.

Pharaoh liked Joseph's plan so well he immediately put Joseph in charge. Thus, in the space of one day, with God working things out, Joseph went from the prison to the palace, from one of the lowest positions in the country to second-in-command behind only the king himself.

In chapter 42 of Genesis, we begin to see where all this might be going. The famine in Egypt also affected Canaan, and Joseph's own brothers were eventually sent by Jacob down to Egypt to buy from Joseph what they could not grow for themselves. Verse 7 tells us that Joseph recognized his brothers the minute he saw them, but Joseph was now in his mid-thirties, clean shaven, and thus unrecognizable to the brothers who'd sold him into slavery when he was only seventeen years old.

How do you think Joseph might have felt at seeing his brothers again?

If ever a man had a chance for big-time payback, this was it. But that, of course, is not how God intended for all this to work out. Chapters 42–46 give us a series of fascinating details of the interchanges between Joseph and his brothers. Here are the main events:

Joseph asked his unsuspecting brothers where they came from. They told him the truth—from Canaan, to buy food. But Joseph wouldn't accept that answer and accused them of being spies, come to see "the nakedness of the land" (Gen. 42:9 NKJV). He then refused to let them go without leaving a hostage (Simeon) behind, whom they could rescue only by returning with their youngest brother, Benjamin, to prove their good intentions. Finally, Joseph had his servants secretly return all of his brothers' money, inside their grain sacks.

On the way home, one of the brothers discovered his own money in his sack, which terrified them all. When they got home things got worse, for then they found that all of their money had been returned. By now they were really afraid, but even so their father, Jacob, refused to let them do as Joseph had required, saying, "You have bereaved me: Joseph is no more, Simeon is no more, and you want to take Benjamin. All these things are against me" (Gen. 42:36 NKJV).

Jacob's resolve lasted until the grain ran out. At that point he had no choice, for there simply was no food to be found else-where. At Judah's urging, he agreed to let his sons return to Egypt, but he advised them to take double the money this time, plus the money they'd found in their sacks. He also agreed, very reluctantly, to let Benjamin go with them—but only after Judah himself offered to forfeit his own life if Benjamin were harmed in any way.

The minute the brothers arrived in Egypt, they went to Joseph's house and talked to one of his stewards at the door, who immediately brought Simeon out to them. When they explained to the steward how they'd found their own money in their grain sacks, he told them not to worry—that God must have done it because he still had the money he'd collected.

At this point the steward took them into Joseph's presence, who inquired about the health of their father and then turned his attention to Benjamin. At that point Joseph could no longer keep a straight face, so he went into another room and wept until he could control himself again. Then he had his brothers served a meal, with their portions taken directly from his own table. But when they were served, Benjamin received five times as much food as the others. Even so, "they drank and were merry with him [Joseph]" (Gen. 43:34 NKJV).

Joseph then commanded his steward to fill his brothers' sacks with grain, to put their money in, too (as before), and to also put his own silver cup into Benjamin's sack. In the morning the brothers loaded their sacks and left, only to be overtaken a few hours later by Joseph's steward. This time, at Joseph's direction, the steward accused them directly of stealing the silver cup, to which they all responded that—if by some miracle he might find such a thing in their sacks—the one who took it should be killed and all the others would willingly become slaves. Then, of course, the steward found the cup exactly where he'd put it, at which point they all returned, once again, to Joseph's house.

Joseph began by essentially lightening the sentence. Rather than death, he would accept Benjamin as a slave for life; the rest could all go home. And then the tide began to turn, and Joseph finally got the evidence he was looking for, that his brothers had changed and were now honorable men. Judah himself pleaded for Benjamin, offering himself in exchange so that Benjamin could return home with the others. Otherwise, said Judah, their father would surely die of grief.

At last it was all too much, and Joseph could restrain himself no more. First he cried out to all his servants and demanded that they leave him alone with his brothers. Then he brought them close and told them who he was—that he was the brother they'd sold into slavery so many years before. At this point Joseph spoke the second-best words of his story, which still serve as an object lesson in the divine providence of God all these centuries later:

> And God sent me before you to preserve a posterity for you in the earth, *and to save your lives by a great deliverance. So now it was not you who sent me here, but God; and He has made me a father to Pharaoh, and lord of all his house, and a ruler throughout all the land of Egypt.* (Gen. 45:7–8 NKJV, emphasis added)

HOW DID JOSEPH PROVE HIS IDENTITY?

Some have speculated that, when Joseph drew his brothers near him, he showed them the one physical proof they could not deny—that he, like all the male descendants of Abraham, Isaac, and Jacob, had been circumcised just as they had. The Bible does not give us specific evidence, but this would certainly seem like a plausible possibility.

When all the above was over, Joseph sent for his father, Jacob, who then moved to Egypt with all his family, plus his flocks and herds. Joseph instructed his brothers to tell anyone who asked, that they were shepherds, so they would be put "far away" from the native Egyptians who considered sheep herding an abomination. Thus they were allowed to settle in an area called Goshen, located in the northeastern part of Egypt where the Nile River empties into the Mediterranean Sea and therefore one of the most fertile areas in that land.

The last portion of chapter 45 details the gifts Joseph gave to his brothers and their father—more than enough to sustain them on the return trip, including changes of clothes and, in Benjamin's case, even three hundred pieces of silver.

What do you imagine that the long-awaited reunion was like between Joseph and his father, Jacob?

How do you think Joseph and his brothers were able to "finesse" Joseph's sudden reappearance? After all, didn't the brothers tell their father that Joseph had been killed?

JOSEPH THE ADMINISTRATOR

Genesis 47:1–12 also tells of Jacob's meeting with Pharaoh, along with a small group of Jacob's sons. Especially endearing is Jacob's comment to Pharaoh, who asked (very politely!) how old Jacob was:

> The days of the years of my pilgrimage are one hundred and thirty years; few and evil have been the days of the years of my life, and they have not attained to the days of the years of the life of my fathers in the days of their pilgrimage. (Gen. 47:9 NKJV)

The last portion of chapter 47 deals with some of the details of Joseph's administrative duties during the famine in Egypt. First he sold grain to the people for money, but eventually they ran out of that, at which point he began accepting livestock instead. When that ran out, and still the famine continued, Joseph gave the people seed in exchange for their land, eventually buying all the land of Egypt for Pharaoh except for what was owned by the priests. Thus Egypt became a nation of sharecroppers, with everyone living on land owned by Pharaoh and contributing one-fifth of all they grew to his treasury.

How do the events in the life of Joseph illustrate God's sovereignty?

The Death of Jacob

Near the end of chapter 47, Jacob asked Joseph to make a vow that, when Jacob died, Joseph would carry him back to the land of Canaan and bury him there. A short while later Jacob became ill, and Joseph visited him with his two sons, Manasseh and Ephraim.

By this time, Jacob could not see clearly, but when he learned who his two additional visitors were he asked Joseph to bring the boys close so he could bless them. He then put his right hand (the hand of the primary blessing) on the younger son's head, and his left hand on the head of the older son, which Joseph attempted to correct.

But even though he could not see, Jacob knew what he was doing. Of the two boys he said to Joseph:

I know, my son, I know. He also shall become a people, and he also shall be great; but truly his younger brother shall be greater than he, and his descendants shall become a multitude of nations. (Gen. 48:19 NKJV)

Jacob also offered a remarkable, threefold description of God as he had known Him . . .

1. The God who was in covenant with Jacob's two ancestors, Abraham and Isaac.

2. The God who had fed him all his life.

3. The Angel who had redeemed him from all evil.

By this act, Jacob participated in the fourth consecutive reversal of the blessing of the younger over the elder—in the last three he was directly involved. The four "reversed blessings" include (1) Isaac over Ishmael, (2) Jacob over Esau, (3) Joseph over Reuben (yet to come at this point), and (4) Ephraim over Manasseh.

Chapter 49 of Genesis contains a long, detailed prophecy by Jacob over his twelve sons, delivered just before he died. The details and the outworkings of these prophecies are beyond the scope of this guide, but they are fascinating in every way. Some came true within a few centuries; others are yet to come true in the end times and beyond.

They also indicate, in Jacob's elevation of Joseph over Reuben (as mentioned directly above), that Jacob was a lot more aware of what was going on, years before, than his own sons knew! Reuben, the eldest, was the one who slept with Jacob's concubine in Genesis 35:22. The same verse tells us that Israel (Jacob) knew what had happened, but apparently he said nothing until the time came to pass on his patriarchal blessing to his sons.

A short while later, when Jacob died, Joseph went before Pharaoh to get permission to make the long, sad trip back to Canaan to bury his father. He then led a huge procession of Israelites back to the land of their ancestry, to lay the bones of their father in the same cave with Abraham and Sarah, Isaac and Rebekah, and Jacob's first wife, Leah.

This was Joseph's first time back to Canaan in thirty-nine years. If he was seventeen years old when he was sold into slavery in Egypt, that would make him fifty-six when his father died.

THE FINAL CHAPTER

As soon as Joseph and his family were back in Egypt, his brothers fell on their faces before him, called themselves his slaves, and begged him to forgive them for what they'd done to him so many years before. At this point, Joseph spoke what many people consider the most memorable words of his story:

> Do not be afraid, for am I in the place of God? But as for you, you meant evil against me; but God meant it for good, in order to bring it about as it is this day, to save many people alive." (Gen. 50:19–20 NKJV, emphasis added)

The last chapter of Genesis ends with the death of Joseph, at one hundred and ten years of age. Like his father before him, Joseph asked the children of Israel to take his bones back to Canaan with them. But unlike his father, he did not ask for an immediate return. Rather, he asked that his bones be taken with them when God delivered His people out of Egypt, saying:

> I am dying; but God will surely visit you, and bring you out of this land to the land of which He swore to Abraham, to Isaac, and to Jacob (Gen. 50:24 NKJV).

Joseph's last request was granted by Moses, as told in Exodus 13:19. And thus the book of Genesis draws to a close.

PULLING IT ALL TOGETHER . . .

• Joseph went to prison because he was falsely accused of adultery by Potiphar's wife. This seemed like a horrible tragedy, but God had a purpose in it all.

• In prison, with God's help, Joseph interpreted dreams for two other prisoners. One of those men eventually remembered what Joseph had done, and recommended him to Pharaoh.

• Joseph interpreted two more dreams, this time for Pharaoh, who immediately took him from prison and made him number two in command over all of Egypt.

• When Joseph's brothers came to Egypt to buy grain, Joseph had an ideal opportunity to get revenge on them for what they'd done to him. But he did exactly the opposite, after testing them to be sure their hearts had changed.

• Joseph reunited and saved his family by bringing Jacob and his brothers down to Egypt, where they were able to survive the famine that might have killed them in Canaan.

• Joseph and his father both lived out their lives in Egypt, but God had other plans for their eventual descendants!

9 COMING TO A CLOSE

A s we tried to make clear in the introduction of this study guide, Genesis is the book of beginnings. But no beginning can be complete without an ending. No one enters a race without intending to finish; no one travels without intending to arrive in the place they were aiming for.

That brings up one of the things that makes the Bible truly unique among all the books of this world—the way in which the beginnings of Genesis are developed and completed later on, in the rest of God's Word. And this is true on both a surface level and on several deeper levels, as well. Let's consider some of the more important threads that begin in Genesis and continue to evolve and develop throughout the remainder of the Bible.

Without question the most important "beginning" of Genesis is the story of the salvation of mankind—and how it can still be accomplished in our lives today. God began to work this one out the minute sin entered His perfect world. His divine solution is explained and amplified throughout the rest of the Bible, via historical narrative, song, poetry, exhortation, prophetic writings, wisdom literature, and any number of additional literary forms and devices.

All of this culminates in the story and the words of Jesus Christ Himself, as recorded in the New Testament. Ironically, the New Testament is often considered the "second half" of the Bible although it accounts for only about 22 percent of the Bible's total word count, minus another 2 percent or so for its 176 direct quotations from the Old Testament.

Nonetheless, the New Testament reexamines, re-explains, recapitulates, reinforces, and most of all verifies and validates all that God tells us in the Old Testament. As for how all this is accomplished . . . well, it's tempting to try to summarize some of these magnificent stories here, but this is simply the wrong place to do so.

In a word, Genesis is the beginning of the story . . . but only the beginning and no more! For example, to find out what happened to the descendants of the twelve sons of Jacob, you must read the rest of the Old Testament historical books.

On the other hand, to find out what happened to the world God created in Genesis . . . well, look around you! Once He created the planets and the rest of the physical universe, He has been content to leave them alone and not tinker with them in any noticeable ways. After all, why fool with perfection?

However, God still allows minor modification of planet Earth, brought about by windstorms, earthquakes, volcanoes, and all the rest of what we call the forces of nature. The universe constantly moves and changes in millions of ways, and thus the physical beginnings detailed in Genesis have their counterparts in constant change even today.

But again, anything that happens now happens in a universe conceived, created, and set in motion by God. He is still the omnipotent Creator, the ultimate Sovereign over all He surveys. All the forces of nature we strive so hard to understand are simply the mechanical methods and means that He originated, in a highly adaptive, yet relentlessly consistent system that no other entity in the universe could possibly create! After all, He is the One who brought all of these things into being by simply speaking the appropriate words. And He is also the only One who could ever maintain such a perfect balance between all those awesome invisible forces and visible objects.

God brought an entire universe out of a formless void. He created all the animal and plant life that exists on Earth. And finally, He created a perfect man and a perfect woman, who then allowed sin and corruption to enter the world by disobeying Him. At that point, God immediately set about to create a means by which man could regain his sinless status, so that he could once again live in eternal, one-on-one fellowship with God Himself.

This above all is the message of Genesis, as it is of the entire Bible. But once again, Genesis is only the beginning . . .

How to Build Your Reference Library

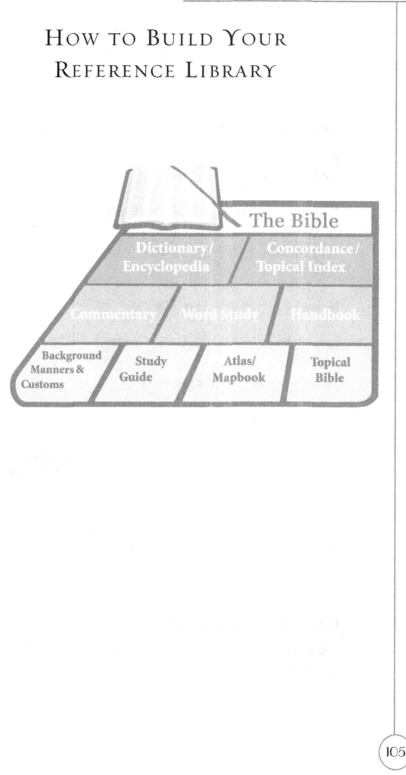

GREAT RESOURCES FOR BUILDING YOUR REFERENCE LIBRARY

DICTIONARIES AND ENCYCLOPEDIAS

All About the Bible: The Ultimate A-to-Z® Illustrated Guide to the Key People, Places, and Things

Every Man in the Bible by Larry Richards

Every Woman in the Bible by Larry Richards and Sue Richards

Nelson's Compact Bible Dictionary

Nelson's Illustrated Encyclopedia of the Bible

Nelson's New Illustrated Bible Dictionary

Nelson's Student Bible Dictionary

So That's What It Means! The Ultimate A-to-Z Resource by Don Campbell, Wendell Johnston, John Walvoord, and John Witmer

Vine's Complete Expository Dictionary of Old and New Testament Words by W. E. Vine and Merrill F. Unger

CONCORDANCES AND TOPICAL INDEXES

Nelson's Quick Reference Bible Concordance by Ronald F. Youngblood

The New Strong's Exhaustive Concordance of the Bible by James Strong

COMMENTARIES

Believer's Bible Commentary by William MacDonald

Matthew Henry's Concise Commentary on the Whole Bible by Matthew Henry

The MacArthur Bible Commentary by John MacArthur

Nelson's New Illustrated Bible Commentary

Thru the Bible series by J. Vernon McGee

HANDBOOKS

Nelson's Compact Bible Handbook

Nelson's Complete Book of Bible Maps and Charts

Nelson's Illustrated Bible Handbook

Nelson's New Illustrated Bible Manners and Customs by Howard F. Vos

With the Word: The Chapter-by-Chapter Bible Handbook by Warren W. Wiersbe

For more great resources, please visit *www.thomasnelson.com.*

NELSON IMPACT™ STUDY GUIDES

The Finest Study Bible EVER!

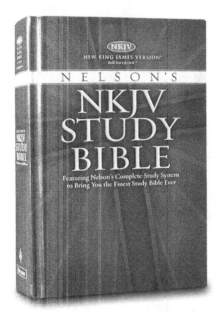

Nelson's NKJV Study Bible helps you understand, apply and grow in a life-long journey through God's Word.

When you want to grow in your faith, Nelson's line of NKJV study tools is all you'll ever need. For more information or to order, contact Thomas Nelson Bibles at 1-800-251-4000 or online at www.nelsonbibles.com

NELSON BIBLES
A Division of Thomas Nelson Publishers
Since 1798

NKJV

NEW KING JAMES VERSION®
Build Your Life On It.™